Offa's Dyke Circular Walks
northern section

Ian Coulthard

Published by Sigma Leisure – an imprint of
Sigma Press, 1 South Oak Lane, Wilmslow, Cheshire SK9 6AR, England.

British Library Cataloguing in Publication Data
A CIP record for this book is available from the British Library.

ISBN: 1-85058-726-4

Typesetting and Design by: Sigma Press, Wilmslow, Cheshire.

Cover photographs: Gyrn from the Offa's Dyke Trail and descending Moel Famau

Cover design: MFP Design & Print

Photographs: Ian Coulthard

Maps: Morag Perrott

Printed by: MFP Design & Print

Disclaimer: the information in this book is given in good faith and is believed to be correct at the time of publication. No responsibility is accepted by either the author or publisher for errors or omissions, or for any loss or injury howsoever caused. Only you can judge your own fitness, competence and experience.

Preface

The Offa's Dyke path, 177 miles long, was one of the first National Trails to be created. This collection of walks is in the longer, northern section between Prestatyn and Knighton. The trail was established in 1971, but the route is continually evolving as diversions are established to improve the quality and safety of the walking. Latterly the popularity of the trail has necessitated diversions or "improvement" of the path to stop increasingly severe erosion, particularly on the dyke itself. All impending diversions, of which I have been advised, have been taken into account in these walk descriptions.

The waymarking of paths on the Offa's Dyke Trail, and other long distance paths which may be utilised, is generally good whilst the level of usage tends to make the way forward obvious. It is sometimes a different matter finding the way along other connecting paths. The Offa's Dyke Path passes through ten different counties and the standard of waymarking varies between counties. Inspired by central government, county councils are opening and waymarking all rights of way but some are making better progress than others, and presently standards can vary dramatically within individual counties. Volunteer groups are also active, and county councils have tended to give priority to the more popular walking areas. It is not surprising, therefore, to find the accessibility of paths noticeably better in areas such as the Clwydian Range, which is designated as an area of outstanding natural beauty.

Several paths have been, or are in the process of being, reopened at my instigation. This has sometimes involved consultation with landowners and local authorities which inevitably delays implementation. At the time these circular walks were checked, shortly before publication, all paths were usable.

The walks in this guide are circuitous and may be started from various points on the route. The start point quoted is a compromise of the availability of readily accessible parking space and having the more energetic elements of the walk in the first few miles. Care is necessary in parking to avoid obstructing large agricultural vehicles in narrow lanes and at access points to fields. I have used "handgate" in referring to small gates, sometimes called wickets, found increasingly on bridleways to allow horseriders to pass through fences without dismounting. I have provided detailed instructions only where considered necessary though information, such as the names of houses or farms, is added as a comfort factor to reassure walkers that they are following the route correctly.

Whilst these walks are predominantly low level the Offa's Dyke Trail undulates – not always gently. There are few walks that involve climbing over 1500 feet above sea level but the height gain may be greater. It is nonetheless relevant to take account of weather conditions both for your own comfort and safety, and to avoid inconvenience to others. Always allow sufficient daylight hours to complete a walk. An allowance of one hour for each two miles plus one hour for refreshment and rest stops will be an adequate provision for regular walkers. A group leader should, however, assess the time required having regard to the abilities of the walking party.

I have been helped every step of the way by my wife, Jan, who has checked the directions by following them on each of the walks. I am also indebted to her for encouragement and enthusiasm in undertaking this project and many practical suggestions, which have improved the end product.

This is the companion volume to walks on the southern section of the trail published in 2000.

Contents

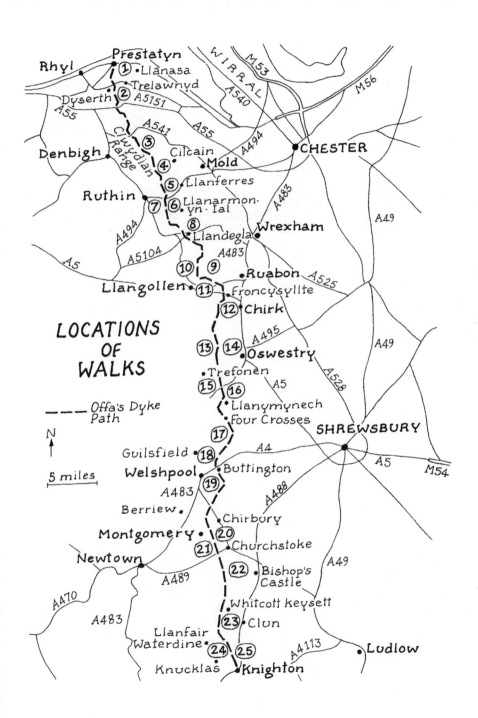

Walk 1: Gwaenysgor and Gop Hill from Llanasa

Starting point: Grid Reference 106815, parking near to the road junction in the centre of Llanasa, which is 2 miles south-east of Prestatyn. The usual approach will be from the A55 dual carriageway about 4 miles south of the village.

Distance: 7 miles (11.3 kilometres)

Height gain: 1100 feet (340 metres) [1300 feet (400 metres) inc. Gop Hill]

Relevant maps: Explorer 265 (Clwydian Range), Landranger 116 (Denbigh and Colwyn Bay)

Facilities: Inns in Llanasa, Gwaenysgor, and Trelawnyd

Terrain: Gradual climb out of Llanasa using enclosed firm tracks with possibly a short muddy stretch before descending over fields to the edge of Prestatyn. Joining the Offa's Dyke Trail, there is a short steep climb on to an escarpment overlooking the coastal plain. The remainder of the walk is generally undulating through fields apart from the optional diversion to the top of Gop Hill. This mound is both a superb viewpoint and of considerable historical interest. There has been speculation that banks on the lower slopes are part of Offa's Dyke.

Llanasa is a very pretty village still maintaining the standard which justified the award for the best-kept village in Clwyd on four occasions in the 1990s. The Church of St. Asaph and St. Cyndeyrn probably dates from the 15th century since when there have been numerous restorations. It is nonetheless attractive with a memorable stunted bell-tower. The font and stained-glass in the east and vestry windows are 14th century indicating an earlier church. A slab in the floor near to the organ is inscribed Grvfvd Vachan (Gruffydd Vaughan), father of Owain Glyndwr who was presumably buried here. Gyrn Castle to the east is a relatively modern edifice of no architectural importance. It was developed by 19th-century industrialists and remains in private ownership inaccessible to the public. Of far greater interest is the imposing well-proportioned three-storey house dated 1645, Henblas, towering over the church and passed at the start of the walk.

1. Go up the lane, signposted to Prestatyn, opposite to the entrance of the church car park and, on the outskirts of the village, turn left along a metalled track. At a junction of paths and bridleways, where the Point of Ayr lighthouse is visible, turn left uphill. The enclosed track deteriorates to a rough stone surface and subsequently grass. Pass a small pool and, opposite the stile to the right, turn left over a stile. Bear right across three fields, following overhead cables, before climbing over two stiles separated by a sandy track.

2. Cross a field as waymarked and another stile at the bottom end of a stone wall. Bear right, but contour across the field as Prestatyn and the coastline up to the Great Orme at Llandudno unfold ahead. Cross the next stile near the bottom corner of the field and converge with the hedge to the right. Climb another stile, walk downhill and then turn left alongside the fence. Cross a stile in the bottom corner of the field, turn right and, after 20 metres, cross another stile into woodland. Go down a clear path to a lane.

3. Continue briefly down the lane and, at the next bend, turn left along the drive to Tyn-yr-Allt. Turn right as indicated by a finger post before reaching the property. Go down steeply through attractively terraced woodland and turn left along a lane for 100 metres. Bear left up a footpath joining the Offa's Dyke Trail.

This point is about one mile from the end of the trail, which runs through the centre of Prestatyn to the beach. Walkers will undoubtedly need to pause for breath once or twice on this steep climb. Above the woodland such stops afford extensive views as far as Snowdonia whilst down below, by following the line of the high street to the coast, the end of the trail can be pinpointed. Prestatyn was a small village until the 1870s when reclamation of the foreshore started. This area was utilised in the 1930s to develop one of the earliest holiday camps, but the coastal area is still flooded by the sea periodically.

4. Continue along the edge of the escarpment to the next finger post and turn left over a stile, leaving the Offa's Dyke Path. Cross the bottom edge of the field and continue down a well-worn

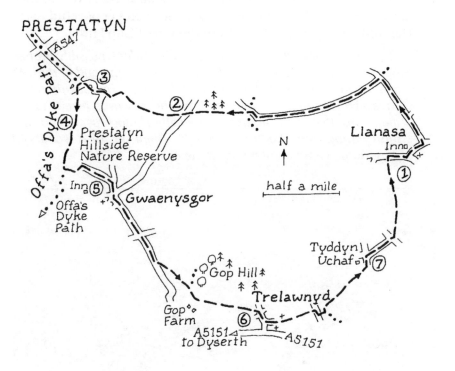

path between hawthorn bushes. Climb a stile and go along an enclosed path, past a spring, into Gwaenysgor. Turn right by a whitewashed stone cottage, Brynffynnon, bearing the date 1680 to pass through the village on the major road.

Gwaenysgor has a small triangular village green with a thought-fully placed seat facing the small church of Saxon origin, which was substantially rebuilt in the 15th century. "Ysgor" means defence – perhaps referring to Offa's Dyke!

5. Having left the village cross the next road junction and, about 300 metres further on, cross the stile on the left by a finger post. Cross two fields, towards the left side of the farm, to climb a stile at the foot of Gop Hill. Turn right to cross another stile and proceed alongside a fence on the right towards a ruined 17th-century stone dovecote. Bear left along a faint track to contour across a large field, at the far end of which a finger post indicates the route of a permissive path to the top of Gop Hill.

The summit mound is the largest cairn in Wales – possibly Bronze Age or even Neolithic – though excavations at the end of the 19th century failed to reveal the secrets of this cairn. Investigation of a cave on the south side at the same time did, however, reveal implements together with the bones of woolly rhinoceros, hyena and man dating from 3,000 to 4,000BC. There are also wonderful panoramic views to all points of the compass.

17th-century dovecot at the base of Gop Hill

6. Continue across the field to a stone stile, follow an enclosed path and turn right towards the centre of Trelawnyd. Turn left along Chapel Street (passing two chapels!) and go forward along a narrow enclosed path between houses. Climb two stone stiles (only 10 metres apart) and one timber stile. Go ahead across two fields and climb a stile in the fence to the left. Continue in the same direction past a pond to a lane and turn right past Cae Glas.

Immediately after passing this house, climb a stile on the left and follow telegraph poles up a field. Climb a stone stile and bear left alongside a stone wall. Cross the stile in the fence ahead and walk up to the crest of the hill. Cross another stile and pass down the right side of a field pock-marked with old opencast mine workings. Climb a stile and go towards the house ahead before turning left along a track – soon enclosed.

7. At a junction of tracks by the entrance to Tyddyn Uchaf Farm turn right down a lane. Turn right past a post box and, after 30 metres, turn left through a field gate by a finger post. Proceed down the left side of a large field towards Llanasa nestling in the valley below. Go through the gate in the bottom left-hand corner of the field and continue down the right side of the next field. Continue downhill and join a track winding between buildings to the road. Turn right past the pond to the centre of the village.

Walk 2: Cwm and Graig Fawr from Dyserth

Starting point: Grid reference 056794, car park near Dyserth Falls, a few hundred metres down the B5119 from the junction with the A5151

Distance: 8 miles (12.9 kilometres)

Height gain: 1050 feet (320 metres)

Relevant maps: Explorer 265 (Clwydian Range), Landranger 116 (Denbigh and Colwyn Bay)

Facilities: Range of facilities in Dyserth

Terrain: Mainly field paths and tracks, some of which are likely to be muddy. The route finding is quite testing on this relatively short walk – care is needed to locate the marker post mentioned in paragraph 3.

Dyserth Falls, only 40 feet in height, are fed from a spring, and historically the waters were believed to have healing properties which therefore attracted pilgrims. Access is by admission at the café.

1. Turn right out of the car park and turn right up Carreg Heilin Lane. Follow the lane bending sharply left and, just before "Rookery Nook", turn sharp right along a footpath. Turn left at a finger post (do not cross the stile), climb a bank and bear left across a field past a marker post. Cross the stile on the edge of woodland to follow an enclosed path and then turn right along a lane to the main road. Go straight on up Foel Road, and bear left along the minor road at the fork. Rejoin Foel Road and, after passing Cobweb Cottage, bear left up a track. Go straight on inside the bottom edge of woodland before climbing progressively along the side of a hill. Later contour along the side of the hill, gradually emerging from the woodland, and cross a sunken lane by way of two stiles.

2. Walk up a field alongside a hedge to the left to cross another stile in the top corner. Go straight on across the next field soon descending steeply to cross a stile at the bottom corner of woodland. Pass briefly through the woods, turn right over a stile and

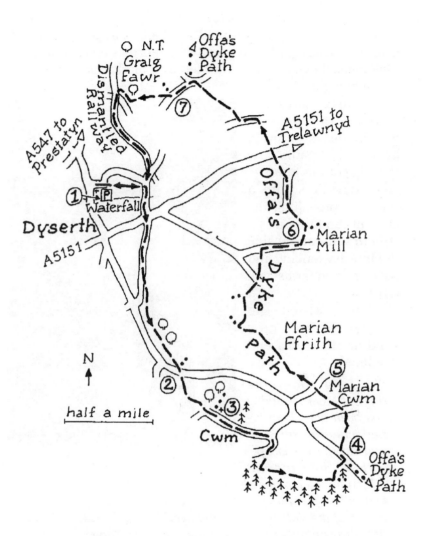

go down the field past a cottage. Turn left along the lane through
Cwm, past the inn and church.

The Church of St. Mael and St. Sulien is built on a steep slope and,
although being all one chamber, it is on three levels. The church is
mostly relatively modern with 14th-century features.

3. Follow this lane out of Cwm for about a half-mile. Turn right at a T-junction signposted to Rhuallt, and after 30 metres, bear left up a waymarked path into woodland. Shortly after the end of the high bank above the path, turn left by a marker post about one metre along an initially faint path (at the time of writing the post is well-hidden by a gorse bush). This path, near the edge of the forestry, soon develops into a track. Approaching the crest of the hill, cross a stile to walk on outside the forestry fencing and past a ruined farmstead. Climb a stile and continue along the clearer track now bending left to descend to a lane.

The long limestone ridge of Moel Hiraddug has been heavily quarried creating an ugly scar on the landscape,

The village church in Cwm

whilst the ancient hillfort on the top has also been largely obliterated. Heavily fortified with stone ramparts, it occupied a commanding position at the mouth of the Vale of Clwyd and overlooking the coast. There are five other hillforts on peaks in the Clwydian Range.

4. Turn left along the lane, joining the Offa's Dyke Trail. 50 metres further on turn right over a stile to cross a large field, containing two Bronze Age barrows, alongside a hedge to the right. Cross a lane by way of two stiles and bear left over the next field towards the small village of Marian Cwm. Cross more stiles and follow the enclosed path into the centre of the village.

5. Bear left across the lane and along a short track. Go straight on over the open ground of Marian Ffrith, prompted by the occasional marker post. Bear right to descend, in the direction of the quarry on the skyline, to cross two stiles before turning left along an enclosed track past a farm. Turn right over a stone stile down a faint track, and pass along the top side of the next field. Turn right down another track and bear left across a lane. Cross a field as waymarked towards a copse, passing to the left of a hedge, and go along the bottom of the next field. Turn right along an enclosed grassy track winding down to a junction by the ruined Marian Mill.

6. Turn left past the fish hatchery and fork right along a narrow lane. Where this lane bends sharply right, go straight on over a stile to the A5151. Bear right across this road, passing around a large farm, to a stile visible at the top of the field. In the next field go straight on down to a lane and turn left. Turn right over the waymarked stile and climb steps to cross a large field, following overhead cables. Cross the ensuing three small fields to turn left down a lane past a cluster of houses, leaving the Offa's Dyke Trail. Climb the stone stile on the right onto the open hillside of Graig Fawr.

> *The peak of Graig Fawr, a limestone outcrop which is in the stewardship of the National Trust, is only 500 feet above sea level but the ground to the north-west is virtually at sea level. The detour to the top therefore provides rewarding views along the coast towards Llandudno and also to Snowdonia.*

7. Continue across the open ground in the same direction as the overhead cables, past the car park, gradually converging with the lane below. Pass through a kissing gate, follow the obvious path alongside the lane down to the disused railway line, and turn left along the track bed. Immediately after passing under a bridge turn left over the bridge along a lane. 50 metres past a junction of lanes, turn right along the path used at the start of the walk to return to the car park.

Walk 3: Penycloddiau and Moel Arthur

Starting point: Grid reference 139668, car park about 2 miles south-west of Nannerch, just before a finger post on the left indicating the Offa's Dyke Trail, along the single track lane signposted to Llandyrnog. Nannerch is adjacent to the A541 Mold/Denbigh road.

Distance: 7.5 miles (12.1 kilometres)

Height gain: 1650 feet (500 metres)

Relevant maps: Explorer 265 (Clwydian Range), Landranger 116 (Denbigh and Colwyn Bay)

Facilities: Pub in Nannerch, full facilities in Mold/Denbigh

Terrain: Largely firm, clear paths and tracks interspersed with fields, across which the route is not so obvious

---

This car park lies on the Offa's Dyke Trail in the valley between Penycloddiau and Moel Arthur, which are both topped by hillforts. Six such Iron Age forts crown hills in the Clwydian Range and most of them are passed or are visible from the walks in this book.

1. Go through the handgate to the rear of the car park and bear right up a forest track, joining the Offa's Dyke Trail. After 40 metres bear right up a narrow path, as indicated by a marker post. Following a stiff climb, cross the stile at the top edge of the forestry and carry on up the ridge to Penycloddiau Fort.

> *The next marker post is adjacent to the outer bank and ditch of the hillfort. This fort is the largest of those in the Clwydian Range, and indeed one of the largest in Wales extending over more than 50 acres. Only the ramparts are clearly visible but the view from the top reflects the superb defensive position of the fort.*

2. Continue along the clear path, punctuated by further marker posts, to the high point of the hill and then descend gradually. After passing a copse of conifers, cross a stile at a junction of tracks and turn right, leaving the Offa's Dyke Trail.

3. At the end of this enclosed track turn right through a gate to follow a clear grassy track through another gate and over a stile. 100 metres after crossing the stile, as the track degenerates to a

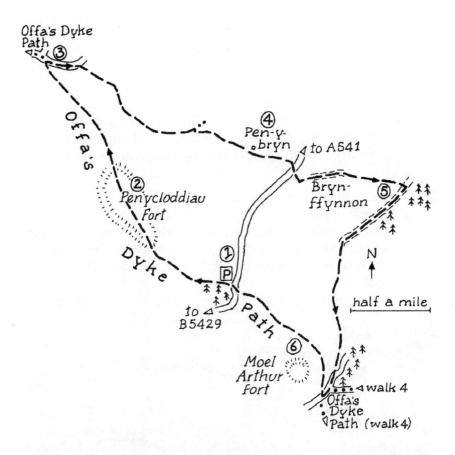

path, fork left to continue alongside fences or walls to the left. Climb the stile in the fence ahead and carry on alongside an old stone wall, past the ruined cottage, to the bottom of the field. Cross a stile and small footbridge, and then converge with the fence to the right. Descend into a valley crossing a stile, a track and passing to the right of an orphan stile. On the other side of the valley cross another stile and footbridge before climbing up the steep bank ahead. Cross a stile by a wooden shed to join an enclosed track and go straight on through the farmyard of Pen-y-bryn.

4. As the track turns left bear right through a gate then turn left. Descend into the next valley, alongside hedges to the left, crossing several stiles, then alongside hedges to the right. Cross the lane in the valley and walk up the track ahead towards Bryn-ffynnon. Follow the metalled track between the houses and turn left over a waymarked stile. Climb directly up the bank behind the houses, cross another stile and bear left up a track. As this track peters out bear slightly left across a large field . Cross a stile, pass through the gate 50 metres ahead and bear right up another large field, towards the right edge of conifers on the skyline.

5. Turn sharply right along a stony track, which gives way to grass at the end of the conifer plantations. Continue along this track for a further mile and bear right briefly along a lane. On reaching a small car park turn right through a kissing gate, rejoining the Offa's Dyke Trail. Follow the well-worn path over the shoulder of Moel Arthur.

On the descent from Penycloddiau *(point number 2)* cross the memorial stile and pass the adjacent stone erected in memory of Arthur Roberts, one of the pioneers of the Trail

There is another hillfort on the top of this hill. There is no right of access but there are "black dotted" paths on the north-west and north-east faces of the hill. This is the most accessible side of the hill and is consequently the most heavily defended with banks and ditches. Bronze Age copper axes were found here during excavations. There is a good overview of this hillfort after the short steep climb at the start of the next walk.

6. Commencing the descent to the start of the walk cross two stiles. Follow the obvious path down to the lane and turn right.

Walk 4: Moel Famau and Cilcain from Moel Arthur

Starting point: Grid reference 147658, car park on the south side of Moel Arthur, along a single track lane 2 miles south-west of the A541 Mold/Denbigh road. The turning (off the A541) is about 150 metres past the lane to Cilcain, when travelling towards Denbigh.

Distance: 7 miles (11.3 kilometres)

Height gain: 1400 feet (430 metres)

Relevant maps: Explorer 265 (Clwydian Range), Landranger 116 (Denbigh and Colwyn Bay)

Facilities: Full facilities in Mold/Denbigh, inn and toilets in Cilcain.

Terrain: Generally firm grassy paths and tracks. An energetic climb to the top of Moel Famau and, at times, an even steeper descent. The latter half of the walk is relatively easy.

The small but superbly positioned hillfort on the top of Moel Arthur was also heavily fortified. Walkers are rewarded with a fine overview after a short strenuous climb at the start of this walk.

1. Leaving the car park cross the track and the right-hand stile to climb steeply up Moel Llys-y-coed, joining the Offa's Dyke Trail walking south. Having climbed up to the ridge of the Clwydian Range, the very clear path continues to wind southwards through typical Welsh hill country with magnificent views in all directions. The trail crosses a track before climbing Moel Dywyll. The path bends sharply left before crossing another footpath where the hillfort, Moel y Gaer, can be seen on the westerly side of Moel Famau. Climb more steeply to the Jubilee Tower at the top of Moel Famau.

> *There are topographs on the tower detailing the surrounding hills and other points of interest. At 554 metres this is the highest point in the Clwydian Range. The tower, built in 1812 to commemorate George III's Golden Jubilee, was topped with an obelisk which was blown over in 1862. All that remains now is the base of the monument which is, nonetheless, a highly visible landmark.*

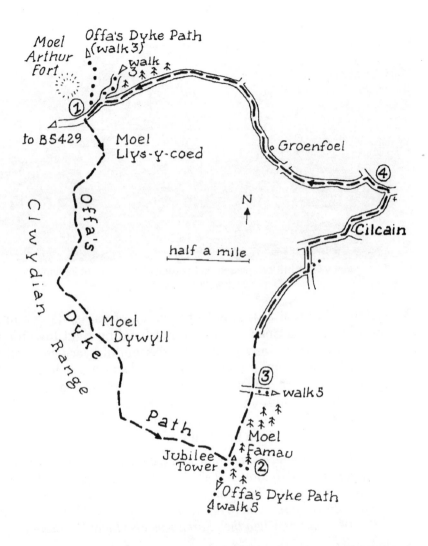

2. There are numerous routes down Moel Famau and care is required at this point to ensure the correct path is followed, leaving the Offa's Dyke Trail. Standing on the tower, face the trig point and then turn left to follow a clear path downhill by a wire fence to the right. This descent is initially quite steep but then more gradual alongside the edge of Clwyd Forest.

Moel y Gaer hillfort, passed on the long climb of Moel Famau
(see direction point 1)

3. Go straight on at a waymarked junction of paths, descending
steeply through open moorland and bending right towards a
reservoir. Join a stony track, now descending very gradually,
and then fork right at a junction of tracks past a marker post.
Pass through a handgate and walk on close by the reservoir.
Cross a stile to join an enclosed track, turning left at the first
T-junction, and right at the second T-junction. Walk down to
meet a lane on a sharp bend and turn left into Cilcain.

*Traditional whitewashed cottages are grouped around the church,
school and pub although there has been some modern development on the north side of the village. The building adjacent to the
lychgate was built to store the hearse – an unusual feature built in
the 19th century, when the church was also heavily restored.*

4. Turn left at the T-junction by the church (unless wanting to
explore further or use facilities in the village) and bear right to
the next junction. Turn left, continue ahead over the ensuing
crossroads along a narrow lane, which later deteriorates to a
track. Follow this fairly level track for well over a mile to a lane
and turn left back to the car park.

Walk 5: Llanferres and Moel Famau from Loggerheads

Starting point: Grid reference 197625, Loggerheads Country Park car park off the A494 Mold/Ruthin road (a popular venue at weekends when the car park is likely to be full at peak times)

Distance: 10 miles (16.1 kilometres)

Height gain: 1950 feet (600 metres)

Relevant maps: Explorer 265 (Clwydian Range), Landranger 116 (Denbigh and Colwyn Bay)

Facilities: Café, toilets and inn adjacent to the car park. Full facilities in Mold/Ruthin and inn at Llanferres.

Terrain: Combination of tracks, open heathland, fields and quiet lanes – mostly firm ground. Route finding for the first third of the walk, until joining the Offa's Dyke Trail, is not always easy. There are three distinct climbs but none are arduous.

The country park offers undemanding walking along the valley of the River Alun using, in particular, the leat created to service the lead mines. This artificial watercourse, extending about three miles, was probably built by a Cornish engineer John Taylor who acquired a number of mines in 1823. The countryside centre has further information on the history of the mining activities which makes interesting reading – disputes over mining rights in the area may even have given rise to the name, Loggerheads.

1. Walk back to the main road and turn right. Immediately after passing the garage cross the road and join an enclosed bridleway. Emerging onto a lane, turn right and, after passing a waymarked stile on the right opposite to a white house, turn left over a stile and go up a clear path along the edge of woodland. Continue straight on through a small field and up a lane past Y Nant.

2. Bear right along a stony track, fork right at a junction and then cross a field to climb the ladder stile in the top corner. Cross the next stile, already in view, and go straight on through scrubland.

Climb the stile in the hedge on the left and contour across a large field as waymarked. Climb another stile, hidden in the hedge beyond a stone wall and beside a water trough. Turn right down an enclosed track for about a half-mile to Llanferres.

Over the road is the quaint Druid Inn with St. Berres Church behind. The inn is the older and more interesting of the two buildings. The church was rebuilt in the 18th century, incorporating an earlier datestone (1650). Inside the church there are slabs/effigies dating from medieval times.

3. Cross the Mold/Ruthin road and walk up Rectory Lane opposite, past the inn. At the end of this lane, after passing houses but before reaching a stile, turn right through a field gate and climb steeply uphill. Turn left through a handgate and contour along the bottom edge of fields. Bear right of a large white bungalow, cross a track and pass through a handgate. Pass through the field gate ahead and another handgate beyond. Contour across another field to join a track through a conifer plantation. Converge with, and join a stony track climbing up from the valley. Walk straight on where the track bends uphill towards Fron-heulog Farm and, emerging from an enclosed section of path, bear left along a faint track.

4. Cross the stile ahead and turn right alongside a stone wall, joining the Offa's Dyke Trail. Climb another stile and follow the fence to the left, then briefly alongside conifers and over further stiles, commencing the climb of Foel Fenlli. Half-way up, at a marker post, bear left to contour over the shoulder of the hill.

The path actually passes along the ramparts of the Bronze Age hillfort built on this hill. There is a permissive path over the top where there is a cairn, also believed to date from the Bronze Age. The hillfort of Moel y Gaer is also visible but can be seen at closer quarters later, when climbing up Moel Famau.

5. Follow the path, punctuated by marker posts, down to and through the car park. Bear left along the major track to undertake the long gradual climb to the top of Moel Famau.

During this climb, shortly after passing a finger post at a junction of

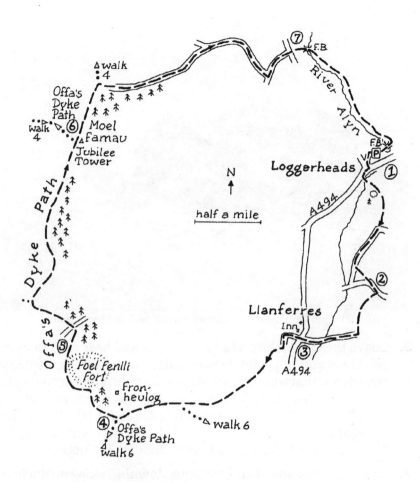

paths, the Moel y Gaer is clearly visible on the crown of a small promontory on the flank of Moel Famau. The more vulnerable east entrance from Moel Famau is protected by offsetting the access through concentric ramparts. Moel Famau is the highest mountain in the Clwydian Range (1823 feet) and the Jubilee Tower on the top was built to celebrate George III's 50 years as King. Unfortunately, the Egyptian-style obelisk on the top was blown down in 1862, and it was only in 1970 that the monument was renovated and modified.

The Jubilee Tower, a landmark on the peak of Moel Famau

6. Leave the Offa's Dyke Trail at the peak and bear right between the tower and trig point. Descend along a stony track in heather moorland, alongside a wire fence to the right, and later along the edge of Clwyd Forest. Turn right at a finger post indicating a junction of paths, initially still along the edge of the forest, then straight on to join an enclosed track. Pass Bryn Ffynnon and turn left at a T-junction down a lane to another T-junction.

7. Cross the lane ahead and continue downhill along an enclosed path (hidden beside the road sign "Loggerheads"). Carry on into the valley, through a field and bear right across a lane. Cross the River Alun, bear right up to another path and turn right along the leat for the last mile of the walk back to Loggerheads. Turn right over the stone footbridge to the Country Park facilities.

Walk 6: Llanarmon-yn-ial and the Clwydian Range

Starting point: Grid reference 187598, lay-by on A494 Mold - Ruthin road adjacent to a road sign indicating toilets 6 miles ahead (in Ruthin)

Distance: 9 miles (14.5 kilometres)

Height gain: 1100 feet (340 metres)

Relevant maps: Explorer 265 (Clwydian Range) and 256 (Wrexham and Llangollen), Landranger 116 (Denbigh and Colwyn Bay)

Facilities: Full facilities in Ruthin and inns in Llanarmon-yn-ial and on the A494 (including one on the route of the walk)

Terrain: Undulating ground utilising paths and tracks. There are some short stretches where the ground may be soft.

The A494 between Mold and Ruthin is one of the few roads crossing the Clwydian Range of hills. Both places are active market towns with attractive old-fashioned main streets.

1. Climb the waymarked stile, between the lay-by and the road sign, to follow the track over the River Alun. Bear right to pass through a field gate where the track again becomes obvious. Ford a stream by way of stepping stones and commence a gradual ascent past old quarry workings. Turn right at a junction of tracks by a large house and continue climbing, as the track evolves into a surfaced lane passing Bryn-yr-Orsedd.

2. Where the lane bends sharply to the right by a modern bungalow, turn left over a stile and follow the clear path by a fence to the right. Go forward over a ladder stile and then cross the stile in the fence to continue in the same direction along an enclosed track. After only 40 metres bear right through a gate to follow another clear path across the open hillside where there are good views of the Clwydian Hills. Join the narrow surfaced lane by Tan-y-Marian and, just after passing a lane on the left, turn left up the drive of Bryn-y-Gloch. Go through a handgate and descend gradually along the lip of a large abandoned quarry.

Carry on past a finger post, indicating a junction of paths, to join a narrow path enclosed by dry stone walls.

3. Cross a road and go straight on along another enclosed path. Turn right down the side of a caravan park and over a stone footbridge, again crossing the River Alun. Climb the stile ahead and then follow the landowner's preferred route to the left around the edge of the field to the top corner. Cross the stile to go along the top side of the next field and then straight on to another stile. Bear right across the last field, past a telegraph pole, to cross the stile in the corner and emerge in the centre of Llanarmon-yn-ial.

This quiet village has declined dramatically since the end of the 19th century, when it could boast ten inns catering for the drovers, quarrymen and miners. Only two quarries remain open but several others are passed in the course of the walk. The double-naved church, dating from the late medieval period but substantially renovated in the 18th and 19th centuries, indicates the size of the congregation in those times. The village is also the birthplace of Elihu Yale, benefactor of Yale University, having made his fortune in America. He is buried in the churchyard of St. Giles, Wrexham, and a replica of the church tower is incorporated into the university buildings.

Stone stile, waymarked "Nurse Fawr", opposite the church in Llanarmon-yn-ial

4. Turn right to follow the road around the church and turn right along an enclosed path, signposted to Nurse Fawr. Pass through a cul-de-sac of bungalows and along another enclosed path. Cross a stile to the left

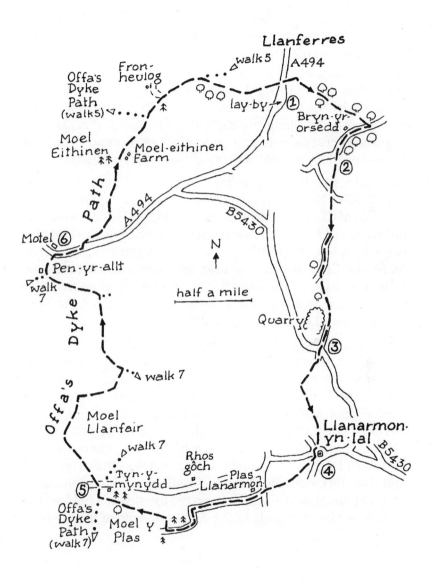

Llanferres

walk 5   A494

Fron-
heulog

Offa's
Dyke
Path
(walk5)

lay-by (1)

Bryn-yr-
orsedd

Moel
Eithinen   Moel-eithinen
Farm

(2)

Path

A494

B5430

Motel (6)

N

Pen-yr-allt

walk
7

half a mile

Dyke

Quarry

(3)

walk 7

Offa's

Moel
Llanfair

walk 7

Rhos
gôch

Llanarmon-
yn-ial

Plas
Llanarmon

(4)

B5430

Tyn-y-
mynydd

(5)

Offa's
Dyke
Path
(walk 7)

Moel y
Plas

and carry on in the same direction up the right side of two fields before crossing the stile on the right in the corner. Bear left towards a farm, passing a marker post on the mound in the middle of the field. Carry straight on up the track beside Plas Farm and around the side of woodland. Immediately after passing a large house by the fishery, turn right to cross two adjacent stiles and turn right again above the conifer plantation. Turn left by the top corner of the plantation along a faint path which contours along the right side of Moel y Plas. Descend slightly to cross a stile and go straight on through woodland. Cross a paddock before turning right down to an enclosed track.

5. Bear left across the track and take the left-hand of the two alternative Offa's Dyke Trail paths, where there is a superb view over the Vale of Clwyd and Ruthin to Snowdonia. After about half a mile turn right up an enclosed track and, nearing the crest of the ridge, turn left over a stile to continue the traverse for a further half-mile. Cross a stile and bear left, past a marker post on a hillock, and bear right down the second field to cross the stile in the bottom corner. Bear right along the track to the A494, opposite the Clwyd Gate Inn and Motel.

6. Turn right briefly along this busy road and, 50 metres after passing the entrance to Bwlch Uchaf, turn left up a stony track. Fork right after 100 metres and go straight on at the next fork for about half a mile. Go forward over a stile as indicated by a marker post, where the track bends right. Carry on along the obvious, fairly level path through the bottom end of a conifer plantation and then descend to a finger post where there is a crossing of paths. Go straight on, leaving the Offa's Dyke Trail, and then fork right along an enclosed track, alongside another conifer plantation. Continue along the top side of a field and join a track, which descends to the A494 opposite to the lay-by.

Walk 7: Moel y Plas from Ruthin

Starting point: Grid reference 126586, car park by the tourist information and craft centre off the A494 on the north side of town

Distance: 10.5 miles (16.9 kilometres)

Height gain: 1400 feet (430 metres)

Relevant maps: Explorer 256 (Wrexham and Llangollen), Landranger 116 (Denbigh and Colwyn Bay)

Facilities: Full facilities in Ruthin

Terrain: Principally firm, clear tracks or quiet country lanes and very easy route finding

Ruthin has an attractive main street running down to the River Clwyd from St. Peter's Square on the crown of the hill. The first Ruthin Castle dates from 1277 and was largely destroyed in the Civil War. The buildings on the same site, now used as a hotel, are early 19th century. Market days are Thursday and Friday. Note the terraced cottages, built in 1864, alongside the old railway line utilised at the start of the walk.

Railway Terrace, alongside the disused railway line in Ruthin

1. Cross the adjacent roundabout and walk along the path, by the side of the A525 Wrexham road, which is part of the old Vale of Clwyd railway line through the town. Turn left along Well Street to a road junction and then follow the minor road sign-posted "Hospital". After passing the hospital, the road becomes a quiet country lane passing through a sandstone cutting. Ignore the minor roads to the left and right, and continue along this lane for about half a mile to a T-junction.

2. Turn right and 30 metres later turn left up an enclosed track, through Bathafarn Farm, forking left by the waterworks. At the next junction of tracks, go straight on up the minor track soon entering woodland. Ignore the level track bending right to a large house and continue uphill, joining another enclosed track alongside the woods. On reaching a small ruined farmstead, follow the track bending sharply left back into the woodland. Emerging from the woods (where there is a good view across the valley to Ruthin) follow the track bending right, which soon passes above a farm to meet the Offa's Dyke Trail.

3. Turn sharp right and cross a stile to climb up the left side of a field, parallel to the Ruthin/Mold road (on the other side of which is the Clwyd Gate Motel). Cross another stile and continue uphill to climb a stile in the top corner of the field. Bear right along the clear grassy track, climbing gradually along the side of the hill. Stay on this track, temporarily leaving the Offa's Dyke Trail, and crest the hill to enjoy the views to the east. Pass through two field gates and carry on along the very obvious track, descending progressively above the top fence of the field system to the left. Go through another field gate to meet the stony track in the valley.

4. Cross the enclosed track by way of two stiles, rejoining the Offa's Dyke Trail, and climb the well-worn path up Moel y Plas. At the top of the hill cross a stile and turn right, alongside a fence, for about 50 metres before bearing left downhill towards a commu-nications mast.

5. Cross a ladder stile when abreast of the picturesque Llyn

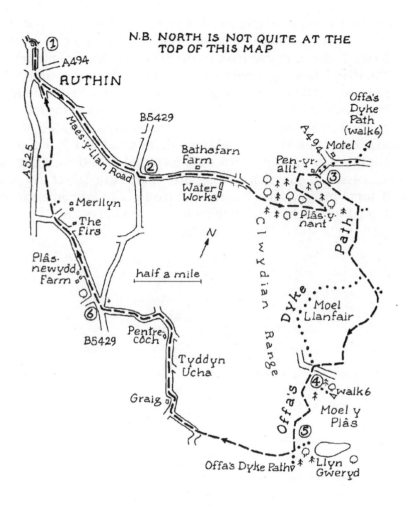

N.B. NORTH IS NOT QUITE AT THE
TOP OF THIS MAP

Gweryd. 100 metres further on bear right down a faint grassy path in the valley, between the previous stile and the mast, leaving the Offa's Dyke Trail. Continue down this valley, above the stream, on a path which becomes much clearer after passing over a stile. Descend to a lane by a stone bridge over the stream and turn right, walking straight on at a junction signposted "Pentre Coch". Pass through this hamlet and, at another road junction, turn left along the lane signposted "Llanfair D.C.".

6. Go over a staggered crossroads and, where this lane bends left, go straight on along an enclosed track. At the end of this track bear left along another lane. At the next bend, by the entrance to "Merllyn", bear right over a waymarked stile to pass along the right side of fields. Approaching a farm, cross the right-hand of two adjacent stiles and walk alongside the hedge to the left. 100 metres further on cross a stile in the hedge to go along the edge of a field and into a housing estate on the edge of town. Bear right to continue in the same direction, turning left and then right at successive T-junctions (along Bro Deg). Turn left at the next T-junction and, after 30 metres, turn right to join an enclosed footpath straight through the remainder of the estate. Turn left, past the hospital, back into the centre of Ruthin.

Walk 8: Llyn Cyfynwy from Llandegla

Starting point: Grid Reference196524, car park in the centre of the village of Llandegla, which is off the A5104 about half a mile north of the junction with the A525.

Distance: 8 miles (12.9 kilometres)

Height gain: 650 feet (200 metres)

Relevant maps: Explorer 256 (Wrexham and Llangollen), Landranger 116 (Denbigh and Colwyn Bay) and 117 (Chester and Wrexham)

Facilities: Pub in Graianrhyd passed during the walk. Full facilities in Wrexham, Llangollen or Ruthin.

Terrain: The first mile is along the valley of the River Alun, initially following the Offa's Dyke Trail, before gaining height using a winding but well waymarked bridleway. The field paths to Graianrhyd include one short boggy stretch. The byway past Graianrhyd Farm maybe churned up by horses or vehicular traffic. A short climb to Llyn Cyfynwy using the right of way is over rough boggy moor and the path is unclear, but a good permissive path is currently offered as an alternative. The lake is popular with fishermen and there are a number of picnic tables, though being the highpoint of the walk, it is an exposed situation. The last two miles involve a gradual descent using mostly obvious firm tracks.

The unusually named St. Tecla's Church, near the car park, was re-built in 1866 in traditional style. The waters of nearby St. Tecla's Well were formerly venerated as a cure for epilepsy, sometime known as the Tecla illness. To the right of the church is a residence which used to be the village pub until the late 1990s, evidenced by the sign – Hand Inn – visible over the front door inside a porch. This walk circles around Bod Ydris Hall, which is about one mile north-east of Llandegla. The hall, largely 16th century but converted into a hotel in the 1970s, may be glimpsed at various stages during the walk.

1. Walk down the track to the right of the church, joining the Offa's Dyke path, and passing to the left of the Old Rectory. Climb a stile and go ahead along the edge of a large field and beside the River Alun. Cross a footbridge over the river and bear right, alongside the fence, to climb a stile in the top right-hand corner of the field. Go on in the same direction to climb a ladder stile and pass along the end of a small conifer plantation. Cross a footbridge and continue ahead for 100 metres, then bear right alongside the river leaving the Offa's Dyke path. Climb two stiles in the fences ahead and bear left away from the river. Cross a stile and footbridge at the left end of a low section of the mature hedge ahead. Proceed up the left side of a field to a lane.

2. Bear right along the broad grass verge and turn right along the enclosed bridleway, indicated by a finger post. Follow the track winding across a field and again cross the River Alun. Bear left around the back of a large farm and climb out of the valley. Sharp turns in this bridleway are well waymarked until approaching a caravan site. Bear right around the edge of this development, where there is a good view of the Clwydian Hills, before turning right along a lane past the house, Rhew Llwyd.

3. At the end of a passing place, and about 100 metres before the lane crests the hill, climb a stile hidden in the hedge to the left and contour across a field below gorse bushes. Climb the high stile in the right-hand corner of the fence ahead, and cross a small boggy field to a lane by the drive to Tyddyn Waen. Go through a gate to the left of the driveway and walk up the field in the direction indicated by a finger post. Cross a stile near the top corner of the field, descend briefly through woodland and bear left in a shallow valley towards the quarry. Pass through a gate in the fence ahead and descend gradually to cross two waymarked stiles. Proceed in the general direction of the telephone box, now in view in Graianrhyd, crossing a stream by way of a footbridge.

4. Turn right along the road and bear right at a road junction, by the Rose and Crown Inn, signposted to Rhydtalog. After passing the pub turn right up a narrow lane and bear left by Graianrhyd Farm up a stony track. At the end of this track[1] turn left along a lane for 150 metres then turn right over a stile, which is on a

---

[1] The stile opposite gives access to a permissive path leading up to the lake. This is both a more direct and easier route.

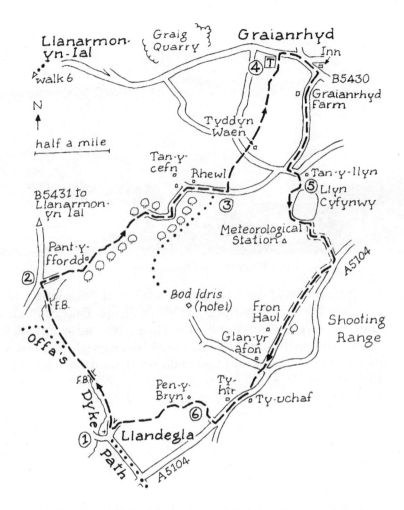

sharp bend in the lane. Climb up open moorland on a faint path, initially alongside a fence, and then straight on to the lake.

This lake is a holding reservoir and licensed fishery stocking salmon and trout. On the hilltop to the right there is a meteorological station.

5. Bear right along the bank of the lake and, at the far end having passed the track to the meteorological station, go along the surfaced track winding down to the main road. Just before

Fishermen at Llyn Cyfnwy

reaching the road, bear right by a brick post box along a faint path towards the finger post on the roadside. Bear right along another waymarked track and climb two adjacent stiles. Proceed down the bottom side of a field diverging from the track. Pass a conifer plantation and walk straight on, through a gate and over a stile, along an enclosed track. Cross an intersecting lane and go through the gate opposite. Continue in the same direction along the less distinct track, passing through two gates, to the A5104. Turn right along this busy road past Ty Uchaf and, 50 metres after the parking sign giving advance notice of the lay-by ahead, turn right down the drive to Pen-y-Bryn.

6. Turn left at a junction before reaching a cattle grid and bear left past the farm. Turn left along the escarpment and cross a stile on the right before reaching woodland. Bear right downhill and then turn sharp left along the bottom of the bank. Ford a stream in the hollow, by way of stepping stones, and then cross a stile. Contour across the top of a small field and proceed alongside the bank past a pond. Cross a stream feeding the pond and bear right, diagonally across a large field. Near the far corner, climb a stile and turn left along a lane into Llandegla.

Walk 9: World's End and Ruabon Mountain from the Panorama Walk

Starting point: Grid reference 247428, follow the signs to the Panorama Walk from the A539 at Trevor, which is 2 miles east of Llangollen, for about a mile. The Panorama Walk is now a lane which contours along the hillside for over two miles. There is a small lay-by on the opposite side of the lane to a large conifer plantation.

Distance: 10.5 miles (16.9 kilometres)

Height gain: 1200 feet (370 metres)

Relevant maps: Explorer 256 (Wrexham and Llangollen), Landranger 117 (Chester and Wrexham)

Facilities: Good range of facilities in Llangollen which has a market every Tuesday

Terrain: Quiet lanes, a traverse principally across scree under the cliffs up to World's End and faint spongy paths on Ruabon Mountain. Route finding on the mountain requires concentration. Paths over the scree are narrow but firm and clear. It is obviously dangerous to stray onto the loose scree.

The Panorama Walk was so named as the resort of Llangollen developed in the late 18th century. It enables visitors to appreciate the beautiful Vale of Llangollen stretching out below. The valley has numerous features of interest – not all visible even from this vantage point. Some are passed in the course of walks in this book including Castell Dinas Bran, Valle Crucis Abbey, Pont Cysyllte aqueduct (the most famous of Telford's prolific building in the valley) the 14th-century bridge over the River Dee, the canal and steam railway. Other sites worthy of detour are Plas Newydd and the Pillar of Eliseg.

1. Join the Offa's Dyke Trail walking along Panorama Walk towards Llangollen, past Castell Dinas Bran, and on for about a mile. Bear right up a stony track, as indicated by a finger post just before Rock Farm, where the lane turns sharply downhill. Carry straight on, where the track bends left into the grounds of a cottage. Traverse the first of several areas of scree before briefly passing through woodland to the road at World's End. This path

Castell Dinas Bran from the Panorama Walk

is very clear but be sure to avoid a path uphill towards the sheer cliffs.

As the road in the valley below converges with the path note the superb 16ᵗʰ/17ᵗʰ-century manor house (Plas Uchaf) at the roadside.

2. Walk up the lane which fords a stream. 80 metres after crossing a cattle grid turn right up the track indicated by a finger post, leaving the Offa's Dyke Trail. Follow a track bending right to join the principal track, climbing gradually along the side of the hill above the forestry for a generous half-mile. Having descended briefly, turn left by a marker post up a narrow but clear path and fork left by the next marker post. At a crossing of paths by another marker post turn right, winding uphill through the heather. Nearing the crest of the broad flat dome of Ruabon Mountain, the path straightens. Descend very gradually towards the right end of a large conifer plantation, above a gully and stream to the right.

3. Carry straight on through the woodland by way of a waymarked

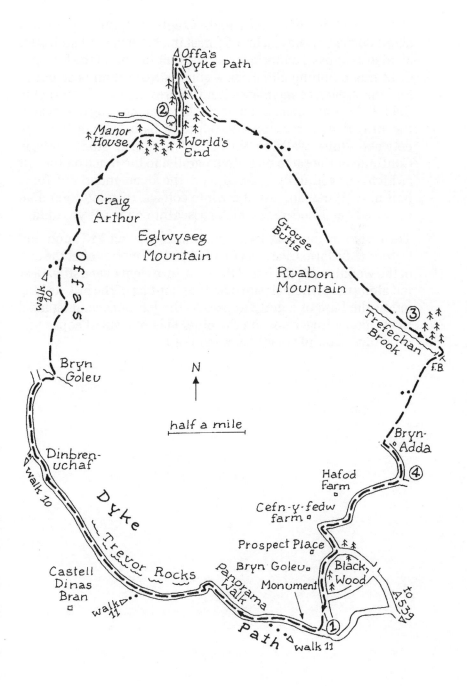

stile. Join a track which descends steeply to a junction of paths about 60 metres above a broad forest track. Turn right and, after 30 metres, cross a footbridge before climbing out of the forestry. Continue climbing alongside a small stream then bear left to ford the stream, as waymarked and before reaching the top of the field. Follow another stream to the left and, nearing the crest of the hill, join a track on the opposite bank. Climb the gate between stone walls to the left of a ruined stone cottage. Continue in the same direction, parallel to the fence on the left (which is eventually crossed), up the open moorland for a half-mile. When abreast of a white cottage, turn left to join an enclosed tree-lined track which passes the cottage, Bryn Adda.

4. Turn right at the next two T-junctions passing Yr Hafod and Cefn-y-fedw farms. Pass Bryn Goleu and, 40 metres after the end of the woodland to the left of the lane, turn right over a stile. Bear left along the principal path over the shoulder of the hill, forking left at the base of a gully to pass to the left of several isolated trees. Pass a finger post on the other side of a small copse and drop down to the lane (Panorama Walk).

Walk 10: Valle Crucis Abbey and the Llangollen Canal

Starting point: Grid reference 198433, picnic site about 300 metres from the Horseshoe Falls on the north bank of the River Dee off the B5103 between the A5 and A542, about one mile west of Llangollen

Distance: 8 miles (12.9 kilometres)

Height gain: 650 feet (200 metres)

Relevant maps: Explorer 256 (Wrexham and Llangollen), Landranger 116 (Denbigh and Colwyn Bay) and 117 (Chester and Wrexham)

Facilities: Full facilities in Llangollen, plus toilet facilities at the picnic site and refreshments at the nearby Chain Bridge Hotel

Terrain: Mainly firm paths and tracks – easy route finding. Undulating ground in a sheltered valley, including one short climb to the Offa's Dyke Trail. A good walk in all weathers with plenty of interest.

This picnic site is adjacent to several well-known features of interest, namely the beautifully situated Horseshoe Falls and Llantysilio Church, the Chain Bridge, Berwyn railway station, railway viaduct and the King's road bridge which spans both the canal and river. These features are all seen towards the end of the walk.

1. Turn right out of the top exit of the picnic site and, after 80 metres, turn left up a track signposted to Valle Crucis Abbey. Follow this track above the road and then bear right, across a lane by a National Trust sign for Velvet Hill, to climb steps by another signpost. Follow a clear winding path over the shoulder of Velvet Hill, still following the path to the abbey at a junction, and descend to the road where the abbey is now in view. Turn left alongside the road for 80 metres and then cross it to go through a kissing gate, where a stone wall bends away from the road. Cross a field towards the abbey, go through another kissing gate and turn left along the track in front of the buildings.

Valle Crucis Abbey was founded in 1201 by the Cistercian Order, which originated in Burgundy in the 11th century. This particular order founded some 85 abbeys in Britain, including 14 in Wales

Valle Crucis Abbey

largely concentrated in the border country. The most notable
feature of this abbey is the west gable of the nave with the window
tracery, including a delicate little rose window. A quarter of a mile
to the north near a lane are the remains of Eliseg's Pillar, now only
8 foot high, from which the abbey takes its name. It is probably
early 9th century topping an older burial mound.

2. Turn right through the caravan site and, where the track bends
left, walk straight on between caravans to cross a footbridge and
climb steps. Turn left along the edge of the bank above the
stream to the end of a large field. Climb a stile, turn right to cross
another stile by a gate and turn left alongside a fence. Follow this
increasingly substantial track for over a mile to a lane and turn
left.

3. At the end of the farm buildings which straddle the lane turn
right through a gate bearing a waymarker. Descend very gradually through three fields to the stream in the valley and cross the
footbridge. Continue along the opposite bank over a stile before
turning left and almost immediately climb another stile. Turn
right to follow the fence passing above a cottage then drop down

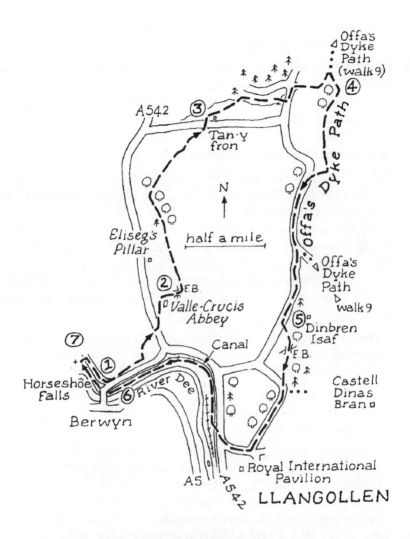

to go along a track to a lane. Turn left along the lane and turn right opposite a barn, just before reaching a road junction, to cross a waymarked stile. Bear left along the bottom of the field past a marker post and cross another stile. Climb steeply up two fields to another stile by a gate, passing a marker post in the gap in the intervening hedge. Cross the stile and bear right for 20 metres before turning left by a marker post over another stile.

Turn right to climb more gradually alongside the fence to the right, and join the Offa's Dyke Trail.

4. As the fence falls away to the right, follow the clear easy traverse across scree and then join a track by a whitewashed cottage. Go forward along a lane for about half a mile and fork right down the lane signposted to Llangollen, leaving the Offa's Dyke Trail. After a further half-mile, cross the stile on the left 100 metres beyond the entrance to Dinbren Isaf.

5. Follow the nearby stream downhill and, after crossing the footbridge over the stream, continue along the opposite bank but before entering a field turn left over a stile. Turn right, to continue in the same direction along the bottom edge of woodland, cross another stile and a track to carry on down steps and through more woodland to a lane. Turn left along the lane and turn right at the next road junction down Tower Road to the A542. Cross the main road and turn right along the canal towpath.

The towpath passes a motor museum and later, the stone embankment of an old tramway which transported slate from quarries above the Horseshoe Pass to the canal.

6. After about a mile pass the Chain Bridge Hotel, where the chain bridge crosses the River Dee, and carry on to the Horseshoe Falls and Llantysilio Church.

The present footbridge over the River Dee dates from 1929, the original crossing having been established early in the 19th century to transfer coal from the canal to the A5. Overlooking the Chain Bridge is Berwyn Station, originally opened in 1865 and still used by the steam railway from Llangollen. The Horseshoe Falls is a misnomer for the weir which was constructed by Telford to divert water into the Llangollen Canal. Continue along the obvious path past the "falls" to the beautifully situated medieval St. Tysilio's Church. The hall in the background was built in Victorian times for C.F. Beyer of Beyer, Peacock & Co. the locomotive builders in Manchester.

7. Carry on up to the road and turn right back to the car park.

Walk 11: Castell Dinas Bran and Trevor Rocks from Llangollen

Starting point: Grid reference 214420, car park in the centre of Llangollen

Distance: 7.5 miles (12.1 kilometres)

Height gain: 1500 feet (460 metres)

Relevant maps: Explorer 256 (Wrexham and Llangollen), Landranger 117 (Chester and Wrexham)

Facilities: Full facilities in Llangollen and inn at Trevor Uchaf

Terrain: Initially a steep climb to the castle overlooking the town, followed by a descent from the mound to join a fairly level stretch of the Offa's Dyke Trail. There is a short steep ascent of Trevor Rocks which is not as fearsome as it looks from below, but care is required not to stray from the path onto loose scree or slip on wet rock when fording the stream. The rest of the walk is virtually downhill all the way. The paths are generally very obvious and firm with a few boggy patches, though the grass on the castle mound is slippery when wet.

Llangollen is still a popular focal point with day-trippers at weekends, but there are several car parks which are usually adequate to meet peak demand. The highlights of the immediate area are the ruins of the castle and Valle Crucis Abbey, Plas Newydd, steam railway, canal featuring the Pont Cysyllte Aqueduct, the Horseshoe Falls and Pass, all in a beautiful setting. The bridge across the River Dee used at the start of the walk is believed to date from 1346 though it has been widened in each of the last two centuries.

1. Walk down the main street (Castle St.), cross the River Dee and turn right. 30 yards later turn left up Wharf Hill, cross the canal and go ahead up the enclosed footpath signposted to Castell Dinas Bran. Pass through a kissing gate and bear right up a field, along the clear surfaced path. Proceed through another kissing gate, in the top right-hand corner of the field, and walk on up an enclosed track. Cross a junction where the path is again signposted to the castle, pass through a further kissing gate and bear

right up the mound to the castle ruins some 750 feet above the town.

This Welsh castle was built in the 13th century on the site of an Iron Age hillfort. The castle was soon reduced to a ruin and abandoned.

2. Follow the well-worn path down the other side of the mound and over a stile. Pass through the kissing gate by a telegraph pole and turn left along a track. Cross a cattle grid and, at a T-junction, turn left down a lane joining the Offa's Dyke Trail. Follow this undulating lane for about half a mile.

3. Turn sharp right opposite to a stile and finger post (leaving the trail for a while) and commence the steep climb up the cliff of Trevor Rocks. The path, initially grassy, soon becomes stony and more distinct but vigilance is needed to avoid straying onto the loose scree. Ford a stream, taking care not to slip on wet or icy rocks, and climb upstream. Bear left through the gap in a stone wall and continue to climb alongside the wall, to a finger post visible on the skyline. Walk straight on at a junction of paths, climb a stile and turn right to contour along the hillside above woodland. Fork right at a junction of tracks and 80 yards later cross a ladder stile in the fence on the right but walk on in the same direction. Pass a marker post, where the walker joins a permissive path rather than right of way. Descend gradually along an increasingly clear path and cross a stile. Continue in the same direction passing a finger post, indicating a junction of permissive paths where there is a glorious view of the Vale of Llangollen and the castle.

The route of the Offa's Dyke Trail for the next three quarters of a mile has again been diverted in 2000, reverting to the path as shown on all OS maps – except Explorer 256 published in 2000! Changes to the route of the trail are being made continually for a variety of reasons such as erosion, and in this case, to avoid an increasingly busy lane (The Panorama Walk).

4. Cross the lane and bear left rejoining the Offa's Dyke Trail, also signposted to Trevor Wood. Follow an increasingly obvious track winding downhill and, just before the gate ahead, turn sharply right down the side of the stone wall. Turn left at the

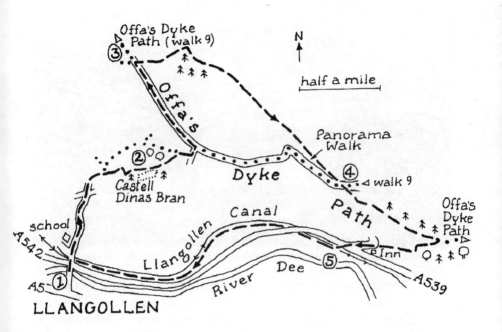

corner of the wall along another track, which narrows to a wood-land path during the ensuing half-mile. Turn sharply right at a waymarked junction of paths, finally leaving the Offa's Dyke Trail. Climb a stile on the edge of the woods and go forward through the gap in an old dry stone wall. Bear left to walk along-side a wire fence around the rim of an old quarry and climb another stile. Turn left down a track which soon bends right. Where the track later bends left go straight on and cross the stile in view ahead. Bear right uphill for 50 metres to a marker post and then fork left as waymarked. Cross another stile by a gate and continue the descent along a track and a lane to the **Sun Trevor Inn.**

Looking back to Trevor Rocks just before rejoining the Offa's Dyke Trail

The canal below between the Horseshoe Falls and the Pont Cysyllte was built as a water feeder for the originally named Ellesmere Canal. After extension of the canal through the Wrexham coalfield to Chester was abandoned, in 1808, the canal was extended to Llangollen in an attempt to make it commercially viable. Thomas Telford's feats of engineering and the path of the canal through unspoilt countryside have now made this canal one of the most popular in Britain for leisure craft.

5. Cross the main road and canal and turn right along the towpath for a mile and a half to Llangollen.

Walk 12: Pont Cysyllte and Chirk Aqueduct from Froncysyllte

Starting point: Grid reference 269414, parking by the community centre off the B5434, about 200 metres from the junction with the A5 in Froncysyllte

Distance: 9.5 miles (15.3 kilometres)

Height gain: 750 feet (230 metres)

Relevant maps: Explorer 256 (Wrexham and Llangollen) and 240 (Oswestry), Landranger 126 (Shrewsbury) and 116 (Chester and Wrexham)

Facilities: Range of facilities in Froncysyllte, and Llangollen. There are also pubs en route near the canal and at Chirk Bridge.

Terrain: Mostly good firm tracks interspersed with field paths. There is a modest climb at the start of the walk, which later passes through two canal tunnels where a torch would be useful. There are numerous features of interest to delay the walker and extend the duration of the walk.

The nearby Pont Cysyllte, taking the canal across the valley, was built by Thomas Telford over a period of ten years and completed in 1805. The cast-iron trough carrying the canal is over a thousand feet long, built on 18 stone piers 120 feet above the River Dee.

1. Walk up the road and turn left along the A5 through Froncysyllte. On the other side of the village turn right, immediately after passing a lay-by with toilets, up a narrow path into woodland. Turn right up a very straight path and then left, more steeply uphill, just before the second line of posts across the path. Cross a stile, leaving the woods, to continue uphill alongside an old hedge line to the left and a copse, at which point there is a glorious view along the Vale of Llangollen. Carry on towards a large tree on the skyline; cross a stile under the tree and contour along the top side of the ensuing field. Cross a stile and walk straight on, along an enclosed track, before turning left down a lane.

2. Continue along this lane for about a half-mile, in the process joining the Offa's Dyke Trail, and opposite a farm turn right over a stile by several gates. Carry on in the same direction over two fields to cross a stile under an isolated tree. Turn right along another lane.

Chirk Castle is now in view to the left, as will often be the case during this walk. This Marcher fortress, built 700 years ago, is still intact and has been continuously occupied since it was built. It is well furnished and beautifully situated in magnificently land-scaped grounds. The Castle is in the care of the National Trust and, of course, open to the public. Between April and September the National Trust allow the use of an alternative path through the grounds, for approximately one mile, before rejoining the official Offa's Dyke Trail. The path through the grounds starts from the lodge on the sharp bend in the lane. The dyke actually passes through the grounds, but has been partly obliterated by an orna-mental lake incorporated in the 18th-century landscaping.

3. Cross the stile to the right of the lodge to continue in the same direction, slightly uphill. Go straight on crossing a succession of stiles and then bear slightly to the right down a track. Before reaching a gateway bear left, past a marker post, to cross a stile in the bottom fence and turn left down an enclosed track. Go through a farm, where the track is surfaced, and continue the descent into the valley. Cross the main road (where the path through Chirk Castle grounds also emerges) to go up the lane opposite over the River Ceiriog. Turn left at the T-junction, leaving the Offa's Dyke Trail, to contour along the side of the valley.

Pass a line of lime kilns on the roadside, which were larger and more substantially built than most and are therefore in an excel-lent state of preservation.

4. Just after passing "The Old School" on the right – now a private residence – turn left down an enclosed track back towards the river. Go through a series of gates and cross a stile, where the track bears right down a field. Cross another stile to follow a clear path through woodland, bearing right at a junction of paths, before descending to the riverbank. Carry on through

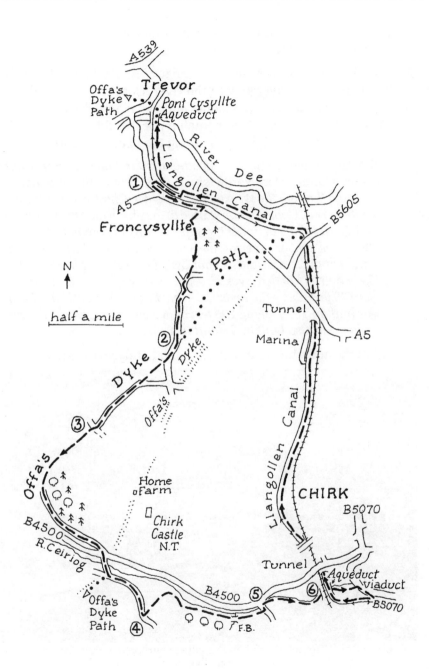

meadows alongside the river, and then briefly ahead along a lane to a junction.

5. Turn left to cross the river again and turn right over a stile, by the T-junction, to converge with the river. Continue alongside the river, under the railway viaduct and canal aqueduct to the A5. Turn right and, almost immediately, bear right uphill past the Bridge Inn to turn right again along the canal towpath.

> *The Llangollen Canal is a dead-end spur from the Shropshire Union Canal near Nantwich. It was originally intended to continue through the Wrexham coalfield to Chester, after crossing the River Dee. Construction started at the end of the 18th century, as canal mania raged, under the supervision of Thomas Telford. The latter was responsible for the construction of Chirk aqueduct, started at the same time as Pont Cysyllte, and completed in 1801. The water is carried over iron plates between stone parapets a mere 70 feet above the River Ceiriog. The adjacent railway viaduct was built in 1848, being 100 feet above the valley, where the road bridge was also built by Telford in 1831.*

6. Cross the aqueduct after which immediately go through the 421

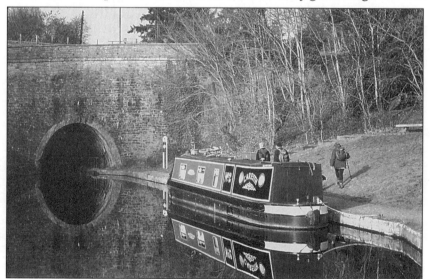

Entering Chirk Tunnel: if you have forgotten your torch, follow the lights of a canalboat

metre Chirk Tunnel. About one mile further on, pass a marina where there will probably be many colourfully painted narrowboats moored. Soon after go through the 174 metre Whitehouse Tunnel. Carry on along the towpath, passing a sign advertising the Britannia Inn where this walk again joins the long distance trail. Cross a footbridge over the canal by the lift bridge, where the Pont Cysyllte Aqueduct is visible (to detour to the aqueduct continue along the towpath). Leave the canal where it bends right to cross the valley and bear right at the road junction back to the car park.

Walk 13: Pen y Gwely and Selattyn Tower from Craignant

Starting point: Grid reference 254350, car park and picnic site on the B4579 near the village of Craignant

Distance: 10 miles (16.1 kilometres)

Height gain: 1200 feet (360 metres)

Relevant maps: Explorer 240 (Oswestry), Landranger 126 (Shrewsbury)

Facilities: Public house in the village of Selattyn and full facilities in Oswestry

Terrain: Very largely firm tracks and quiet country lanes – consequently easy route finding. There are three very moderate climbs, two of which are in the latter third of the walk on the Offa's Dyke Trail.

The car park is in old limestone quarry workings – and there are the remains of kilns in the valley below. Soon after leaving the car park, the dyke crosses the road and continues across the bottom of the valley. At the roadside there is a stone wall dating from the 19th century incorporating an inscribed stone tablet.

1. Turn left out of the car park and walk along the lane to a sharp bend. Go straight on along a track winding up the valley ahead. Continue straight on, leaving the principal track where this bends left, to the head of the valley. Cross another track and, after another 100 metres, follow the track bending sharply right up to and then around a farm. Pass between the original farm buildings and the new farmhouse, following the obvious track between conifers to a lane. Turn left along this lane, joining the Glyn Ceiriog Trail.

> *The Glyn Ceiriog cycle trail is a waymarked circular trail some 23 miles long. Further west there is another cycle trail 14 miles long called the Upper Ceiriog Trail.*

2. Fork right at a road junction and continue along this lane for about three-quarters of a mile, enjoying the views over the Glyn Ceiriog Valley. At the end of a conifer plantation to the right,

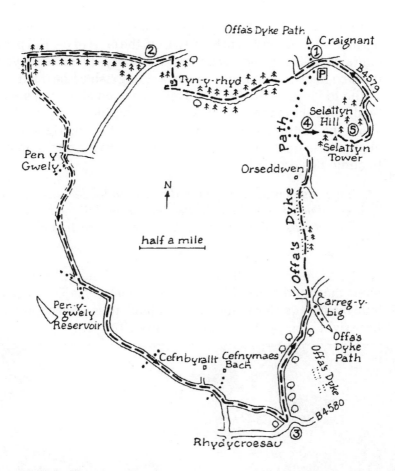

turn left along a cross-track. This track winds across the shoulder of Pen y Gwely (to the right) and descends to a lane by a farm. Turn left down the lane and then turn right down a waymarked bridleway at the side of the farm. After passing the farm, bear left at a fork in the tracks and walk on for the best part of a mile. At a crossing of tracks, where the Glyn Ceiriog Trail is waymarked straight on, turn left. Join another very clear track, which winds around the side of the hill ahead for a further mile and evolves into a lane. Pass the entrance to Cefnymaes Bach and turn left down a narrow lane to a T-junction.

3. Turn left over a stone bridge and then left again along another narrow lane signposted to Selattyn. On the crest of the hill pass a lane signposted to Old Racecourse Oswestry. 30 metres beyond the next road junction, and opposite riding stables, bear left over a stile to join the Offa's Dyke Trail. Carry on along the side of fields and along the edge of woodland beside or on the dyke. Cross the footbridge over a stream before turning right briefly along a farm track. At a junction of tracks turn left and soon start to climb Selattyn Hill.

> *The dyke is now several hundred metres to the left, occupying a classic defensive position on the side of the hill facing Wales – indeed on this hill it still marks the border between England and Wales.*

4. At the corner of woodland near the top of the hill turn right along the top edge of fields, leaving the Offa's Dyke Trail. Cross a stile by the gate ahead into the woodland, pass a finger post and bear right along a clear path to Selattyn Tower.

Selattyn Tower, partly restored

This is a Victorian folly, recently rebuilt, which would have been visible for miles around and is also sited inside an ancient stone circle. The significance of the viewpoint is unfortunately lost in the dense woodland but there is still an extensive view on emerging from the trees.

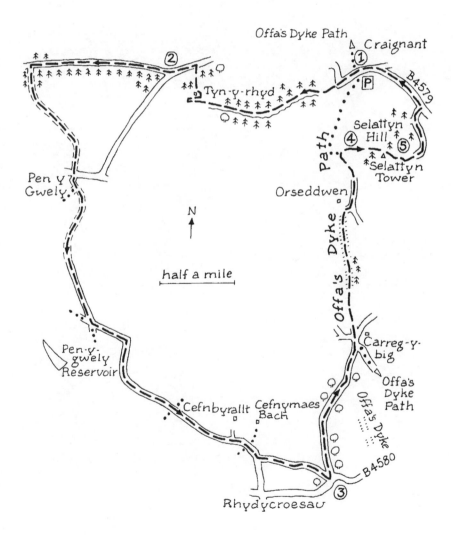

5. Carry on along the clear path and cross the stile ahead at the edge of the plantation. Walk down fields firstly alongside woodland, and then by stone walls to the right before joining a track. Follow the track bending left, as indicated by a finger post, and then proceed along the bottom edge of woodland. Join a stony track descending to the lane and turn left back to the car park.

Walk 14: Brogyntyn Hall and Old Oswestry Hillfort from Oswestry

Starting point: Grid reference 294300, car park in the centre of Oswestry near the bus station

Distance: 9.5 miles (15.3 kilometres)

Height gain: 900 feet (280 metres)

Relevant maps: Explorer 240 (Oswestry), Landranger 126 (Shrewsbury)

Facilities: Full facilities in Oswestry

Terrain: Principally firm tracks interspersed with quiet country lanes and field paths. The first half of the walk involves a gradual climb to Old Racecourse Common, followed by the descent through Brogyntyn Park. Route finding is generally very easy except for the first part of the descent from Old Racecourse Common, which is an ideal place for a picnic lunch.

Traditional-style shops in the town centre struggle for survival against the obvious competition of two modern supermarkets by the car park. St. Oswald's Church, with its imposing tower, is visible from virtually anywhere in the town. The tower dates from the 13th century whilst there are 17th-century timber-framed houses nearby in Church Terrace and Llwyd Mansion in Cross Street. What little remains of the 12th-century castle is on a mound behind the town hall, both passed at the start of the walk. Of greater interest are Brogyntyn Hall and Old Oswestry Hillfort, both passed on this walk.

1. Leave the car park at the top end, by the conveniences, and walk up the road to the town centre (as indicated by a finger post). Bear right to pass to around the left side and rear of the town hall and pass the castle mound. Go down Chapel Street and turn left to the staggered crossroads. Cross Willow Street and continue along Welsh Walls, turn right down Brynhafod Road and then turn left along Jennings Road. Turn right at the T-junction up Oswald's Well Lane, past the well.

2. Continue up this road and turn left along a track by the water-works to turn right up another road. After 100 metres turn left across a waymarked stile and pass to the left of the mound at the

far end of the field. Climb a stile and continue in the same direction to converge with and join a faint track.

3. Cross a lane to continue along the track, now more obvious, through parkland later bending right uphill towards woodland. Cross the stile ahead and bear right across a clearing to find a short marker post (at times obscured by undergrowth), indicating a junction of paths, and turn left. Follow the path, bending left alongside an old walled garden, and continue in the same direction over a field. Cross a stile into another large area of parkland and bear left to join a faint level track, passing to the right of the fence around a tree bearing waymarkers denoting a junction of paths.

4. Cross the stile to the right of the farm ahead and follow the track between the farm and woods. After 40 metres bear right up a broad path, then go straight on past a marker post and turn right at a junction of tracks. Fork left at the next junction of tracks and continue along this track, past a marker post, to a crossing of tracks. Turn right for the long climb to the ridge above the woodland, having joined the Offa's Dyke Trail. Leave the woodland briefly and as the path levels out pass through a conifer plantation and onto Old Racecourse Common.

5. Turn right, leaving the Offa's Dyke Trail, and follow the waymarked path partly on the old racecourse. Turn right off the racecourse at a marker post and pass a house, named "Domo". Cross the stile ahead to go down the side of a field to a junction of lanes and turn right down the principal lane. Turn left through the first field gate encountered, which is about 300 metres down this lane, to walk directly away from the lane. Bear right to pass through another gate between two mature trees in the bottom corner of the field and continue through further fields alongside hedges to the left. Join an enclosed track which leads to a very straight road, where the traffic is likely to be fast-moving.

6. Proceed along the lane opposite and turn right down a track towards a farm. Continue along the major track, passing to the left of the large block of farm buildings, and across Brogyntyn

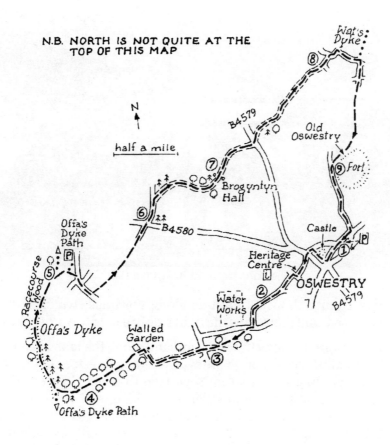

N.B. NORTH IS NOT QUITE AT THE
TOP OF THIS MAP

Park between mature trees. Carry on through woodland and pass down the side of Brogyntyn Hall.

This mansion, which was the family home of Lord Harlech, dates from 1730, having been enlarged progressively during the following 100 years, and is a grade II listed building. Most noteworthy is the Ionic portico on the south façade. The hall has been empty for some years now and is showing the evidence of having been abandoned to the elements.

7. Carry on down the main drive through the park to the gatehouse and bear left across a lane to join a waymarked track. Bear right along a stony track to the right of the walled garden of an attrac-

The Doric façade of Brogyntyn Hall

tive country house. Continue along the track, which is later enclosed, and then along the right side of a field towards a farm.

8. Go forward through the farmyard and along the lane ahead to a T-junction. Turn right to follow a winding lane for about half a mile, passing the drive to Yew Tree Cottage. Go straight on towards a farm at the next left-hand bend, and cross the stile ahead. Bear right to cross another stile by a gate in the fence soon after passing the farm. Continue in the same direction with a hedge to the left, having joined the route of Wat's Dyke, towards Old Oswestry Hillfort. Bear right around the hillfort and turn left along a lane which passes the entrance to the fort.

> *This is an outstanding example of an Iron Age hillfort established about 600BC– it is also one of the largest in the country covering an area of some 40 acres. Wat's Dyke, like Offa's Dyke, is also believed to date from the 8th century. It was built to the east of Offa's Dyke in the Oswestry area, but it is a smaller earthwork and is therefore less obvious nowadays.*

9. Carry on along the lane into Oswestry, going straight on along Llewyn Road, to a T-junction which is within sight of the car park.

Walk 15: Moelydd

Starting point: Grid reference 256278, small lay-by at a junction of lanes by a sign for the "Old Mill Inn" and an Offa's Dyke Trail finger post. This junction is two miles south-west of Oswestry on the Llansilin road (take signs for Trefonen / Llansilin out of Oswestry and turn right signposted to Llansilin by another sign for the "Old Mill Inn"). Please do not obstruct the gateway in the lay-by.

Distance: 8 miles (12.9 kilometres)

Height gain: 900 feet (270 metres)

Relevant maps: Explorer 240 (Oswestry), Landranger 126 (Shrewsbury)

Facilities: Full facilities in Oswestry, inn at Trefonen and Old Mill Inn near the start/end of the walk

Terrain: Largely field paths and quiet country lanes or tracks. There are two modest climbs, to the top of Moelydd and through the Craig Sychtyn Reserve. A few short boggy stretches may be encountered.

From the lay-by there are extensive views to the north over woodland through which the Offa's Dyke and trail climbs up to the old racecourse. There is also a good view to the east over Oswestry. The first half-mile of this walk passes along an outstanding section of the dyke.

1. Walk back to the road junction and turn right over a stile, joining the Offa's Dyke Trail. Later follow the path along the top of the dyke and then in the same direction on the other side. Bear left across a lane before continuing in the same direction. When abreast of the stile in the hedge to the left, turn right to cross another stile at the bottom of the field. Bear left over another lane and follow a track, and later enclosed path, to the village of Trefonen.

2. Go straight on through the top end of the village to a T-junction and turn right. Go straight on, as the lane bends right, and along the right side of a field. Cross several stiles and a footbridge in the hollow to go straight on up the next field. Pass two isolated trees, cross a stile and turn left along a lane briefly. Turn right at the next junction up a narrow lane. Pass a farm and woodland, as the lane deteriorates to a surfaced track. Cross the stile ahead on a left-hand bend and climb up the side of a large field, initially on another track. Turn left at the finger post by a farm and soon bear right up a track, crossing a stile as the track bends sharply right. 50 metres further on leave the track, bearing right up a grassy path, past marker posts, leading to the top of Moelydd.

Whilst only 285 metres above sea level this is a splendid viewpoint. The Berwyns can be seen to the north-west possibly covered with a dusting of snow in the Winter. In fine weather this also makes a good stop for lunch.

3.   Turn sharply left and descend, as indicated by the finger post, then turn left along a track. Pass Ty-uchaf and cross the stile in the fence on the right, leaving the Offa's Dyke Trail. Follow the clear path down two small fields and climb another stile. Turn right alongside the fence, descending gradually, in the process of which cross a stile and walk on alongside a hedge. At the bottom of the hill cross two stiles and bear left to a white house. Climb the stile in the corner of a field by Bron-y-nant and turn left down a lane. Cross a ford and follow the lane steeply uphill to a T-junction by Ffynon-deg.

4.   Turn left briefly and cross the stile on the right to continue climbing alongside the cottage. Bear left at a marker post and walk towards unfenced mature trees, without losing height. Cross a stile in the edge of the woods and descend to a junction of paths. Turn right to follow a clear fairly level path, ignoring another waymarked path climbing away to the right. At a junction of paths after a short descent, turn right and enter the Craig Sychtyn Reserve.

There are information boards at both ends of this small reserve showing, in particular, the position of the quarry and limekilns. The coppiced woodland would, of course, have provided the fuel for the kilns. This is a site of Special Scientific Interest noted for the plants and birdlife.

5.   Follow the path along the bottom of the reserve and then a track

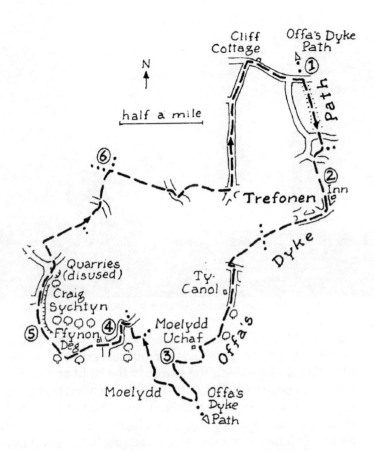

gradually ascending. Where the track descends bending left, climb the stile on the right to cross a field below the small limestone quarry and remains of a limekiln. Cross a lane and walk up through a copse before bearing left along the contour towards a farm. Turn right along the second side of the same field and then continue in the same direction, now with a fence to the right. Cross a stile and bear left down an L-shaped field and then over another lane. Bear left across fields and stiles, gradually bending right to a junction of paths by a stream.

The view towards the Berwyns from Moelydd

6. Turn right over the stream and climb the next field. Cross another two stiles close together and carry on in the same direction. Climb the stile in the hedge to the right and walk on now with the hedge to the left. Cross a stile between two gates and go forward down a lane. Cross the stile on the left and climb again, joining a track leading through a farmyard to a lane. Turn left along the lane, signposted to Croesaubach, for about half a mile and turn right at the T-junction to return to the lay-by.

Walk 16: Llanymynech Hill and Llynclys Hill Nature Reserve

Starting point: Grid reference 265209, car park behind the Dolphin public house off the B4398, signposted to Llansantffraid-ym-Mechain, near the junction with the A483 in the centre of the village

Distance: 6 miles (9.7 kilometres)

Height gain: 600 feet (180 metres)

Relevant maps: Explorer 240 (Oswestry), Landranger 126 (Shrewsbury)

Facilities: Full facilities in Oswestry, public houses in Llanymynech and Llynclys

Terrain: Just one fairly easy climb in the first mile and straightforward route finding, except in and just beyond the nature reserve. The ground on the hill and towpaths is firm but low-lying fields may be muddy.

The village straddles the border between England and Wales and the main street also follows the route of Offa's Dyke. The hill above the village has obviously been quarried for limestone. The site of the kilns and tramways by the canal and railway line has been developed as a heritage area. Less obviously, however, the hill has been mined since Roman times to extract lead, copper and zinc. In the interest of personal safety, walkers should stick to the well-waymarked Offa's Dyke Trail up to the golf course.

1. Cross the stile at the end of the car park and turn right along the towpath. Pass under the road and turn right up steps to walk up the road, joining the Offa's Dyke Trail. After about 150 metres bear left up a lane, signposted to Pen y Foel, and later fork right at a junction of lanes by a post-box. At the end of this lane, now roughly surfaced, bear left over a stile into the Llanymynech Rocks Nature Reserve. Cross another stile and, at an intersection of paths, turn left to climb steeply to a T-junction of paths and turn left. A few metres further on fork left and then bear right to climb obliquely up the side of the hill, where there are extensive panoramic views to the south. Leave the nature reserve by way of a handgate and bear left along the edge of a golf course, also alongside the dyke.

2. Follow marker posts, to avoid straying onto the golf course, and then carry on along the ridge in or beside woodland to a junction of paths by an orphaned stile. Go straight on along the ridge, leaving the Offa's Dyke Trail, past a particularly good viewpoint on the edge of Blodwel Rock. Go down steps to cross a stile, and bear right across a clearing below "The Firs", entering the Llynclys Hill Nature Reserve. On the other side of the clearing turn left down a well-used bridleway. Shortly after, at an intersection of bridleways, fork right continuing alongside a dry stone wall and as waymarked by a blue arrow on a marker post. Go straight on, descending gradually, to a major intersection of paths and tracks by a cottage, and turn sharply right along the stony track.

3. Follow this track, bending left then right, before crossing the waymarked stile on the left, and descend through woodland along a faint path. If in doubt, bear right to stay on a broad ridge. Pass through a clearing, and then bear left along a broad path (which converges with overhead cables) between trees to climb a stile. Bear left across the corner of a field, diverging from the overhead cables, to cross two adjacent stiles in the broad band of scrub which creates the field boundary (care required here as there are another two stiles over the fence higher up the field!). Go straight on down the middle of the next field towards the nearest house, noting the marker post visible by the hedge in the next field. Carry on, past this post and the house, along the edge of fields and then down a driveway to the A483 at Llynclys.

4. Turn right at the road junction, signposted to Knockin, and cross the bridge over a dismantled railway line noting the old station building to the left – with a lovely garden where the track bed used to be. 50 metres further on climb the stile on the right by a finger post. Cross the middle of a field as indicated to climb a stile clearly visible in the hedge opposite. Bear left to climb another stile by a telegraph pole in the top hedge and then bear right along the bottom edge of further fields. Continue in the

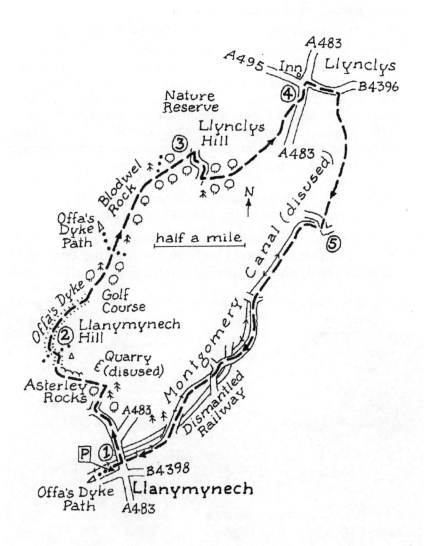

same direction across the next two fields, to reach a lane by a hump-backed bridge over the currently disused branch of the Shropshire Union Canal.

The Montgomery Branch was closed in 1936 when there was a major breach near the junction with the Llangollen Canal at Lower Frankton. Until recently it had been assumed that this branch would never be reopened but the popularity of canal boating has generated the enthusiasm to reopen the canal. At the time of writing the six mile stretch from Lower Frankton to Maesbury Marsh, and the land-locked stretch around Welshpool are open. There is a substantial amount of groundwork to be done, particularly where the canal has been filled in for road improvements. It remains to be seen whether the money will be found to complete the project. Don't be confused by the milestones, cast in the belief that the towpath was on the other side of the canal!

5. Cross the bridge; turn left down to the towpath and pass under bridge alongside the canal bed. On reaching the next bridge leave the canal, where the towpath is currently impassable. Bear

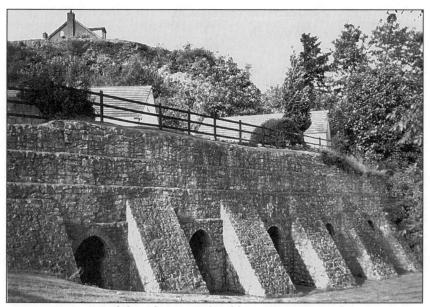

Limekilns adjacent to the old Montgomery Canal

left away from the canal along a quiet lane which soon bends right, running parallel to the canal. After about a third of a mile this lane converges with canal again enabling walkers to rejoin the towpath which can be followed back to the car park.

Half-way back to Llanymynech this section of towpath passes between the pillars of a dismantled railway bridge. Presently it is possible to cross the canal and climb up to the old railway track bed, which runs parallel to the canal into the village. It is not, however, a right of way and access may not always be allowed. There is an information board about the limestone quarrying, which developed firstly because of the canal and then the railways. The site between this point and Llanymynech has been developed as a Heritage Area and is the more interesting route. Walk towards the brick chimney and climb the steps from the track bed to the base of the chimney where there are two conventional limekilns, and also a rare Hoffman horizontal ring kiln. The latter is in an excellent state of preservation having been built in 1899 and only used for 15 years before the demise of the industry on this site.

Walk 17: Derwas Bridge and Four Crosses from Arddleen

Starting point: Grid reference 261158, lay-by on the west side of the A483 at the southern end of Arddleen

Distance: 7.5 miles (12.1 kilometres)

Height gain: 50 feet (20 metres)

Relevant maps: Explorer 240 (Oswestry), Landranger 126 (Shrewsbury)

Facilities: Full facilities in Oswestry, pubs in Arddleen and Four Crosses

Terrain: Very flat (nominal height gain), and generally firm ground apart from a couple of farmyards which may be muddy

---

This walk, at the time of writing, involves crossing the A483 on four occasions. Two of these crossings may be eliminated in the fullness of time by the renovation of the Montgomery Canal. Road improvements undertaken since the canal was closed to traffic eliminated weak and narrow bridges, which was the most cost-effective option at that time. Such road crossings are now the major impediment to the re-opening of the canal.

1. At the southern end of the lay-by, cross the stile to join the canal towpath. Follow the canal for about half a mile to bridge 104 and turn left to the T-junction. Turn right down the lane away from the bridge and past a farm. Cross the bridge over a broad drainage ditch and climb the stile on the left to walk along the embankment. Cross the track bed of a dismantled railway, where this bridged the ditch, and walk on to the main road.

2. Cross this busy road with care and, passing through the gate opposite, carry on along the embankment. Cross a quiet lane and continue ahead for about a mile past two other crossings of the ditch and a junction of ditches.

   At Derwas Bridge join the footpath utilised by both the Offa's Dyke Trail and the Severn Way as indicated by the finger post bearing the acorn long distance trail motif.

3. Cross the bridge and bear right over a large field, as directed by

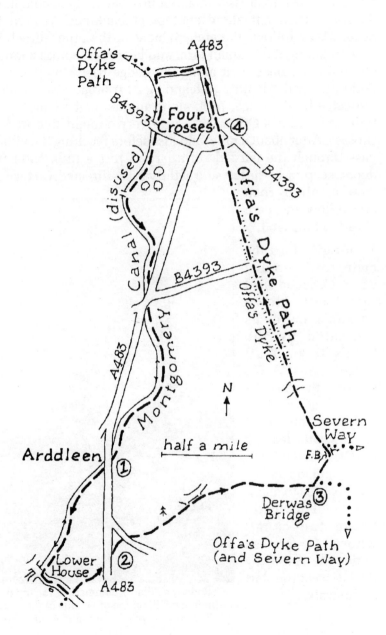

the finger post, to cross a small footbridge barely visible in the distance. Turn left along another embankment (where the Severn Way follows the embankment in the other direction). Pass to the right of a small farm and bear right across a lane to climb a stile. Bear right along the hedge past a marker post. Follow the hedge bending left and then turn right over a stile, as indicated by the finger post, along another embankment. The trail now follows Offa's Dyke in a very straight line to Four Crosses. After about a mile, and just before reaching the village, pass through the left side of a farm. Cross a milk collection depot, keeping to the left side of the yard as directed. Go forward over a minor road and follow the path ahead to the A483.

4. Turn right along the main road through Four Crosses and turn left down Parson's Lane, as indicated by the Offa's Dyke Trail finger post. Go through the farm at the end of the lane and turn left along the towpath, leaving the Offa's Dyke Trail. Bear right on crossing the A483 to rejoin the canal towpath. Leave the canal, where it passes under the A483, by the lay-by at the start of the walk.

Rodney's Pillar, a landmark at the top of Breidden Hill on the other side of the River Severn, and visible throughout this walk

Walk 18: Guilsfield and Pool Quay from Buttington Wharf

Starting point: Grid reference 242089, Buttington Wharf picnic site at the junction of the A483 and A458

Distance: 9 miles (14.5 kilometres)

Height gain: 250 feet (80 metres)

Relevant maps: Explorer 240 (Oswestry) and 216 (Welshpool and Montgomery), Landranger 126 (Shrewsbury)

Facilities: Full range in Welshpool, public houses in Guilsfield and Pool Quay

Terrain: Principally quiet country lanes, green lanes and canal towpath. Easy route finding and no ascent of significance.

There is an old lime-kiln between the car park and the canal wharf, now a picnic site. At the time of writing this section of the Montgomery Canal is land-locked following various road improvement schemes after the canal was abandoned. Restoration, started in 1969, is proceeding slowly but surely to reopen the original canal running for 33 miles from Welsh Frankton to Newtown. The towpath is utilised as part of the Offa's Dyke Trail.

1. Cross the bridge, adjacent to the wharf, over the canal and walk up the narrow lane. Ignore a minor right turn and soon leave the houses behind as the lane deteriorates to a rough track. At a road junction go down the lane opposite and carry straight on at a junction of tracks. Pass to the left of Plas Trelydan down a green lane, where the ground tends to be very soft and then progressively improves on nearing Guilsfield. Turn right along the main road into the village.

The massive tower of St. Aelhaiarn's Church looms ahead, having been in view for some time. The tower is all that remains of the 12th-century church, most of which dates from the 15th century. Memorable features include the original door, lean-to building at the side of this door to store the hearse, and lovely ceiling. There are houses representative of the 17th, 18th, and 19th centuries both

Don't be confused by the mileposts, obviously cast in the belief that the towpath
was on the other side of the canal!

adjacent to the church and dotted around the valley. A branch of
the Montgomery Canal intended to extend to Guilsfield was never
completed.

2. Turn right opposite the church along Arddleen Road and then
turn right down Cemetery Lane. Bear left down Folly Lane and
go straight on at the next junction. Bear left past Folly Farm
(rather than following Folly Lane to the right), admiring the
black and white 17th-century farmhouse.

3. About 200 metres further on turn left down a lane past the
3 tonnes weight limit sign. Follow this lane bending right and
then go straight on at the next junction. Continue along the track
for about a mile, at the end of which turn right along a lane.

4. Cross the canal and turn right along the towpath for three miles
back to Buttington Wharf. This towpath is joined at Top Lock by
the Offa's Dyke Trail and Severn Way but the Offa's Dyke Trail
subsequently leaves the towpath about one mile before reaching
the wharf.

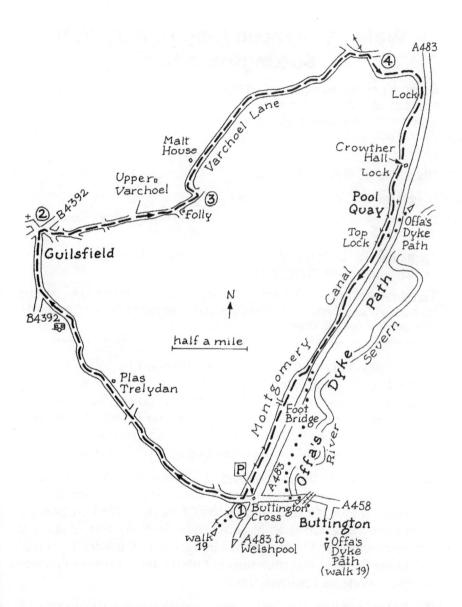

The River Severn passes very close to the canal at Pool Quay and this was an important point of transhipment, being the highest reach of the river which was navigable.

Walk 19: Beacon Ring Hillfort from Buttington Wharf

Starting point: Grid reference 242089, Buttington Wharf picnic site off the roundabout at the junction of the A483 and A458 (alternative starting point – car park by information centre and adjacent to the canal in Welshpool). *Please note that the path through the Leighton Estate used on this walk is closed on Ascension Day.*

Distance: 9 miles (14.5 kilometres)

Height gain: 1100 feet (330 metres)

Relevant maps: Explorer 216 (Welshpool and Montgomery), Landranger 126 (Shrewsbury)

Facilities: Full facilities in Welshpool and public house in Buttington (on the other side of the River Severn)

Terrain: Initially field paths with a few boggy patches, then firm tracks and towpath. A fairly long but gradual climb up to the hillfort before the equally gradual descent into Welshpool.

The Montgomery Canal, connected with the Llangollen Canal at Welsh Frankton and extending 33miles to Newtown, was originally constructed between 1792 and 1821. This section of the canal is currently land-locked following the canal being breached and abandoned in 1944. Restoration, by British Waterways and various voluntary groups, has been proceeding slowly since 1969.

1. Walk down to the roundabout and along the A458 Shrewsbury road. Cross the bridge over the River Severn and immediately turn right over a stile, joining the Offa's Dyke Trail, to cross the railway line. Go straight across two fields by way of stiles in view ahead and bear right of a bungalow to the road. Turn right along the road and then turn left up the far side of the business park along an enclosed track.

2. Before reaching the ditch ahead turn right over a stile to proceed diagonally up fields, the direction clearly indicated by the readily visible stiles. Cross a stone slab over a ditch and bear left up the side of the next field but revert to crossing the following

A renovated section of the Montgomery Canal in the centre of Welshpool

field diagonally. Climb a stile to follow the track, winding up to the right of a farm, to a cottage. Cross the stile on the left to bear right across a small field. Climb another stile and proceed directly uphill, past marker posts, to a lane.

3. Bear right across the lane to climb another stile and continue up the right side of fields and an enclosed track. Where the track enters a field, fork left uphill and in the following field bear right to climb a stile.

> *Look back at this point where there is a superb view across the valley, Welshpool, Powis Castle, and the Welsh Hills to Snowdonia.*

4. Continue to the crest of the hill, following the fence to the left and then bear right to contour across a large field towards the top corner of a forestry plantation. Enter this dense woodland by way of a stile to follow a clear path. Turn left along a track which reverts to a path again just inside the boundary fence. Cross a stile and turn right around the perimeter of the earthworks.

These are the remains of Beacon Ring hillfort, an Iron Age fortified settlement. The trail follows the still substantial single rampart but it is a pity that a forestry plantation was established inside the hillfort in the 1950s.

5. Having walked halfway around the fort turn right, as waymarked, over a stile to start the gradual descent alongside a fence to the right. Cross the stile in this fence and continue in the same direction down the side of a plantation, on the other side of which, turn right by the boundary fence. At the bottom of the field go straight on down a track to a road junction and turn right, leaving the trail. Where the lane narrows turn left down a track into the Leighton Estate, to descend along a stony track through the woodland. Turn right at a junction of tracks by Hollybush Cottage. Carry on downhill past Old Cable House, ponds, and Leighton Farm to a T-junction by Tafolog.

    The Leighton Estate was developed by a Liverpool banker, John Naylor, in the mid-nineteenth century. In addition to the model farm the path passes ponds which were part of the elaborate water collection system. The church with the tall spire, a landmark frequently visible in the latter part of the walk, was built at the same time as Leighton Hall.

6. Turn right along the road, utilising the broad grass verge, and turn left down a waymarked track to Gravel Lodge. Cross the bridge over the adjacent stream, and go through the gate to the left of Gravel Lodge. Pass through fields by the River Severn following an embankment. Go forward through a gate, along the side of Severn Lodge, and turn left along the road over the river into Welshpool. Go straight on at the roundabout to cross the footbridge over the railway and by-pass. Continue in the same direction towards the town centre (past a modern stone circle which commemorates an "eisteddfod").

    The old Victorian railway station is built in the style of a French chateau. Welshpool is a large market town attractively laid out with some handsome buildings. Tourist features include Powisland Museum and Canal Centre, the Welshpool and Llanfair steam railway and, one mile south of the town, Powis Castle and

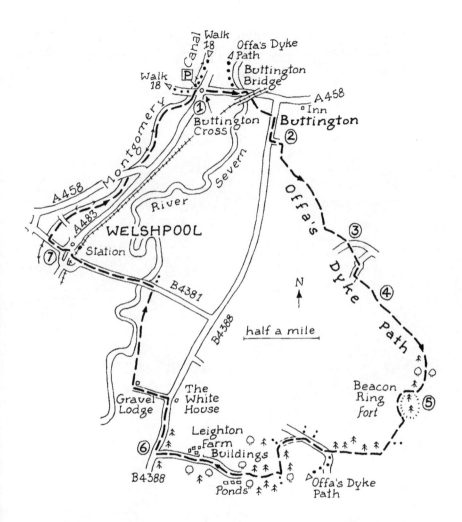

gardens. The latter was originally a Welsh castle dating from the 12th century but has been developed by successive generations of Herberts and Clives (of India!).

7. Bear right through a small grassed area to turn right along the canal towpath, crossing the small aqueduct over Lledan Brook (the nearby bridge leads to the main car park and information centre). Follow the towpath, bearing right across a road, where the canal has been re-routed under the road. Rejoin the towpath, passing under a further two bridges, to return to Buttington Wharf.

Walk 20: Marrington Dingle from Chirbury

Starting point: Grid reference 262984, car park in the village off the A4386 Marton road

Distance: 7.5 miles (12.1 kilometres)

Height gain: 250 feet (80 metres)

Relevant maps: Explorer 216 (Welshpool and Montgomery), Landranger 137 (Ludow, Wenlock Edge)

Facilities: Full facilities in Montgomery and hotel in Chirbury

Terrain: Principally field paths interspersed with tracks, some soft ground will probably be encountered. The walk is in a lowland area near the River Camlad and the height gain is therefore minimal. There is however quite a steep descent into Marrington Dingle.

The walk starts from a delightful Shropshire village with a substantial ex-priory church dating from the late 13th century, though greatly altered during 18th and 19th-century restorations. Also note the school, built in 1675, south-east of the church and the picturesque inn by the church.

1. Walk through the village along the A490 Welshpool road, past the hotel and church. 100 metres after crossing a narrow bridge turn left over a waymarked stile, opposite to a converted red brick barn. Follow the obvious track across a field and then go forward along the left-hand side of a hedge. Approaching a farm, bear left to pass through a metal handgate between the farm and cottages. Bear right along a track through the farm.

2. After passing all of the buildings, turn right over a stile and cross two further stiles in quick succession. Pass diagonally down the next field to cross a footbridge under a large oak tree. Proceed alongside a fence to join a track to the right of another farm and go straight on at a junction of tracks. Bear right in the next field, still on the now faint track, to a gate in the corner of the field and turn right along an enclosed track.

The road twists and turns around the old buildings in Chirbury.

3. Turn left by a cottage, just before reaching the stile ahead, and join the Offa's Dyke Trail. After about 50 metres turn left through a handgate to walk alongside the dyke for about one and a half miles, crossing to the other side where indicated by a marker post. The trail crosses a lane after the first half-mile and later continues alongside the woodland of Lymore Park.

> *Walk number 21 starts from Montgomery – one of the jewels of the border country. There is a good view of the town, castle and war memorial at the top of Town Hill from the dyke. There are a number of older forts on the same hill emphasising its strategic importance from the Iron Age to medieval times.*

4. Leave both the trail and the dyke by turning left along a metalled track by a cattle grid. Stay on the track, bearing right by a farm to go through three gates close together, and then fork left through a further gate as the track divides. Pass through another gate by two large trees. At the adjacent marker post bear right over a field, leaving the track. Cross a stile and bear right to follow the hedge and climb another stile in the far corner of the field. Cross

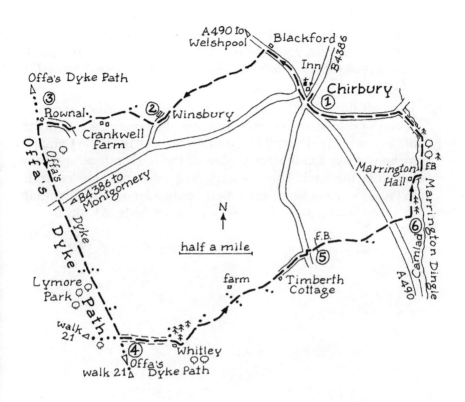

a track, which leads down to a farm, and continue in the same direction across an exceptionally long field. Join the track just below an isolated house.

5. At the end of this track turn left along a lane for just 30 metres and climb the stile on the right. Cross two small fields and a foot-bridge in the hollow. Ascend briefly, past an old cottage, and continue in the same direction in the next field. Cross a stile under a large tree before bearing right towards agricultural buildings in the distance. Climb the left-hand of two stiles, which are 50 metres apart in the hedge ahead, and carry on up the side of a field to cross the A490. Continue in the same direction over stiles to a fence bounding woodland in a valley, called Marrington Dingle.

The black and white Marrington Hall is now visible on the left. The border country abounds with old timber-framed houses of which Marrington Hall, dating from 1595, is an outstanding example. It is not open to the public but this footpath affords the best view of the house.

6. Turn left alongside the fence, walking towards the hall, and then cross the stile in the fence. Continue in the same direction to the old water-mill in the valley. Cross the leat and the River Camlad, by way of two footbridges in front of the mill-cottage, and turn left along the track. This track climbs briefly and then descends to cross the river again and emerge onto a lane. Turn left along this lane which joins the A490 on the outskirts of Chirbury.

Walk 21: Town Hill and Lymore Park from Montgomery

Starting point: Grid reference 223965, the town hall square (if this is full use the car park on the south edge of town off the B4385 – barely 250 metres from the centre)

Distance: 6.5 miles (10.5 kilometres)

Height gain: 600 feet (180 metres)

Relevant maps: Explorer 216 (Welshpool & Montgomery), Landranger 137 (Ludlow, Wenlock Edge)

Facilities: Full facilities in Montgomery

Terrain: Mainly tracks and quiet country lanes, interspersed with field paths which may be muddy. Very flat terrain after the short climb, which can be omitted, to the top of Town Hill.

Montgomery is an old county market town historically important as evidenced by the imposing town hall. The 20th century, and particularly the major road network, has left the town centre largely un-

The town hall, one of the many handsome old buildings in Montgomery

touched. There are, consequently, numerous historic buildings to be admired – each bearing a small but highly informative plaque – and the town is now one of the border country's hidden gems.

1. Facing the town hall, leave the square by the top right-hand corner, walk along Arthur Street and then turn left opposite the ironmongers up the waymarked path to the castle.

   Established by Henry III in the 13th century, this castle was largely dismantled in 1649 after the Civil War. Its commanding position on a promontory, overlooking the town and surrounding country-side in three directions, can nonetheless be appreciated. There are sites of three older forts on high ground to the west which were established to control an old ford across the River Severn, nearer which there is also the site of a Roman fort.

2. Follow the level path to the castle car park and turn right to the lane. Go along the waymarked path opposite and after 25 metres bear left along a fairly level path (following the line of the old town ditch). Converge with and join a stony track. At a finger post bear right up the ridge to the monument in view at the top of Town Hill.

   This is a war memorial, situated by the trig point, where there is a commanding view of the surrounding countryside from this high point at only 320 metres above sea level. The various peaks in the distance are detailed on the nearby topograph.

3. Return downhill the same way and then turn sharp right along the track, carrying on through fields alongside hedges to the left. Bear left through a gap in the hedge and follow the hedge bending right, as indicated by a marker post. Climb the stile ahead and turn left along an enclosed track which descends to a narrow lane (ignore tracks running off to the left). Turn left at each of the ensuing two T-junctions. Turn right up a waymarked enclosed track to Weston Hill Farm and cross the stile straight ahead. Carry on along the edge of three fields to cross two stiles in quick succession by a ruined cottage. Bear right by the fence to the next gate and turn left alongside a ditch to emerge onto a lane by a cottage. Turn right and then fork left by a post box

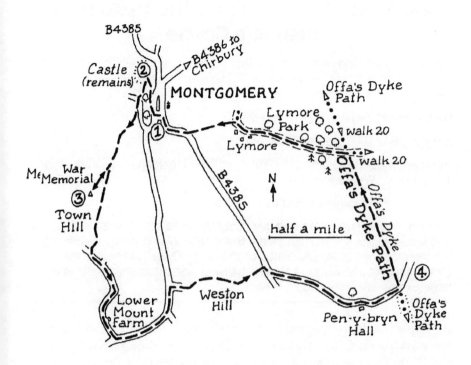

down a narrow lane, past Pen-y-bryn Hall, to Offa's Dyke and the trail.

The dyke runs almost due north in a very straight line across the broad flat valley and the long distance footpath follows alongside.

4. Turn left along the trail for just about three-quarters of a mile to a surfaced track and turn left along this track, which passes through Lymore Park, towards Montgomery. Pass a large grouping of farm buildings and turn left along the waymarked bridleway which emerges on the B4385, by the car park on the edge of town mentioned in the preamble.

Walk 22: The Church on the Dyke from Bishop's Castle

Starting point: Grid reference 324886, main car park in Station Street except on market days – Thursdays, Fridays and Saturdays – when parking may be a problem

Distance: 12.5 miles (20 kilometres)

Height gain: 1600 feet (490 metres)

Relevant maps: Explorer 216 (Welshpool and Montgomery), Landranger 137 (Ludlow, Wenlock Edge)

Facilities: Full facilities in Bishop's Castle

Terrain: Mainly firm tracks and quiet country lanes interspersed with fields and forestry. The first section on the Shropshire Way is gently undulating but there are two energetic climbs on the Offa's Dyke Trail before the gentle descent into Bishop's Castle. Utilising well-established trails to a large extent, the route finding is easy.

Bishop's Castle, by-passed by the main road, is an excellent centre for walking on Offa's Dyke or the Stiperstones/Long Mynd area to the East. The rectangular street plan of the town is typically Norman. There are a number of buildings dating from the 16th century including the "House on Crutches". There are museums, breweries, antique and craft shops together with numerous shows, fairs and a variety of hostelries – some providing evening entertainment. Little remains of the castle established in the 12th century by the Bishops of Hereford, when they were also powerful Marcher Lords, on the hill above the town now dominated by the Castle Hotel.

1. Walk down the main street towards the church. Bear right around the large church down Church Lane, joining the Shropshire Way, and turn right along Field Lane. This lane soon bends left and degenerates to a stony track. Pass a cluster of houses and go straight on over a stile, where the surface changes to grass before reverting to stone. Where this track bends left down to a farm, walk straight on along the bottom edge of fields and then descend towards another enclosed track. Do not join this track

The lovely little church on the dyke

but turn right to follow the stream up the valley for about three-quarters of a mile, crossing numerous stiles.

2. Turn left along a track, bending right opposite to the entrance to a farm. Climb gradually to pass through the right side of another larger farm. At a junction of enclosed tracks above the farm bear left and, at the end of this pretty green lane, carry on along the bottom edge of a field. In the next field turn left alongside the fence to cross the stile at the top of the field and turn right alongside a fence. Go through gates, passing a barn, and turn left along a lane for 50 metres. Turn right along a very straight green lane which climbs progressively to the crest of a hill. Go through a gate on a left-hand bend to descend along another very straight stretch of green lane with a fence to the right. From the top corner of a large field carry straight on and, at the intersection of tracks in the bottom corner, turn left. At another junction of tracks, at the bottom end of the field, turn right through a gate along another enclosed track to a junction of lanes by the entrance to Reilth Farm.

3. Go down the lane opposite to cross the River Unk and immediately turn right along a clear path through woodland. Where the broad path starts to ascend bear right to climb two adjacent stiles and cross a meadow to the far bottom corner. Turn left along a lane and, almost immediately, turn left again to climb briefly up a narrower lane. As this lane straightens out bear right over a stile by a gate to follow a level path through woodland for about a half-mile. Pass above the church, cross two stiles and descend through a new conifer plantation to the church, leaving the Shropshire Way and joining the Offa's Dyke Trail.

> *"The Church on the Dyke" nestles in the valley in the small hamlet of Churchtown. St. John the Baptist Church was rebuilt in the late 19th century but has retained the splendid Elizabethan oak roof and panelling.*

4. Cross the lane and stile to start a steep climb, past a marker post and over another stile ahead. The trail now follows a particularly prominent section of the dyke for about one and a half miles. Cross a track and a lane before descending to cross the footbridge over a stream in a lovely valley. Bear left along the track for 100 metres and then turn right over a stile to climb through Nut Wood, crossing another track. This climb is less severe than previously and, emerging from the woods, bear left along the boundary fence and then the dyke. Cross the dyke, as indicated by a marker post, and climb two stiles onto a lane by the entrance to Crows Nest. Turn right along this lane, leaving the both the dyke and trail, immediately joining the Kerry Ridgeway for the gradual descent into Bishop's Castle.

> *The Kerry Ridgeway is 15.5 miles long, extending from Kerry to Bishop's Castle, and follows the ancient drovers' route from Wales to the English markets.*

5. After about half a mile cross a junction by a telephone box and after a short climb note the ancient hill-fort of Caer Din in the field on the left. At the next junction of lanes one mile further on follow the lane signposted to Bishop's Castle. After a further half-mile, turn right down the lane signposted to Lydbury North, leaving the ridgeway. After another mile pass a farm and,

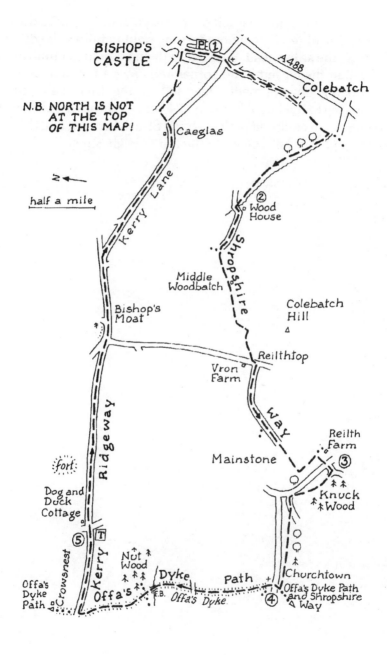

at the next bend, bear left over a waymarked stile. Go down the left side of the field before turning right to follow the ditch and cross the stile ahead. Bear left in the next field to climb another stile in the far left-hand corner and cross a field into a modern housing development. Bear left at the first road junction, passing to the left of house no.74, and go through a kissing gate. Follow an enclosed path to Union Street, turn left and then right through Market Square to the top of High Street.

Walk 23: Graig Hill from Clun

Starting point: Grid reference 300808, Clun Bridge car park adjacent to the ancient bridge over the River Clun in the centre of the village

Distance: 10.5 miles (16.9 kilometres)

Height gain: 1600 feet (490 metres)

Relevant maps: Explorer 201 (Knighton and Presteigne) and 216 (Welshpool and Montgomery), Landranger 137 (Ludlow, Wenlock Edge)

Facilities: Full facilities in Clun

Terrain: Tracks, field paths and quiet country lanes. The walk starts with the gradual ascent along a broad ridge before an undulating section in the middle of the walk and a gentle descent to Clun. Ground conditions are generally firm.

Clun is renowned for both the medieval bridge and castle dating back to Norman times. The substantial earthworks and four-storey keep are the only recognisable remains of this border fortress which suffered major attacks in 1196 and 1233, and was abandoned by the 15th century.

1. Cross the footbridge behind the conveniences and climb up to the castle. Leave the castle grounds by way of the main entrance near the bowling green and immediately turn left over the stile, joining the Shropshire Way. Follow the clear path alongside the hedge to the right, and then on the other side of it, to a track. Go forward along this track, which soon becomes a green lane, to the end. Cross the footbridge over a stream and turn right over a stile to follow the stream, crossing another footbridge and a stile. After walking briefly along the bank of the stream go forward along another green lane for about a half-mile.

2. Bear right across a lane to commence the long steady climb of about one and a half miles along a broad ridge. Pass up the side of two fields before bearing right as indicated by a finger post. Go past a marker post and cross a stile; carry on up the left side of a field to climb another stile and bear left across a green lane to join an enclosed path. Go forward up the right side of fields,

The remains of the castle in the village of Clun

reassured by waymarking on stiles, to the crest of the ridge. Watch out for a waymarker directing walkers to bear left diagonally over a field to climb another stile. Follow the hedge bending left and join a track, initially enclosed, descending to a cluster of farm buildings in the valley.

3. Join a lane and turn left at the crossroads, signposted to Mardu, leaving the Shropshire Way. Follow this lane descending for a generous half-mile, keeping to the right at junctions. Turn left at a junction with an Offa's Dyke Trail finger post on the corner, which is 30 metres before the driveway to Lower Mount. After 75 metres, turn left across a stile. Cross the nearby stream and another stile to bear right along the side of Graig Hill (do not follow the path descending to the bank of the stream).

4. Approaching a farm, cross a stile in the hedge at the top of a field to follow a track uphill briefly and then walk straight on, fording a stream. It is now obvious that the path is along or adjacent to the dyke for the next one and a half miles, until leaving the trail at Springhill Farm. Follow the dyke over the shoulder of Graig

N.B. NORTH IS NOT AT THE TOP OF THIS MAP!

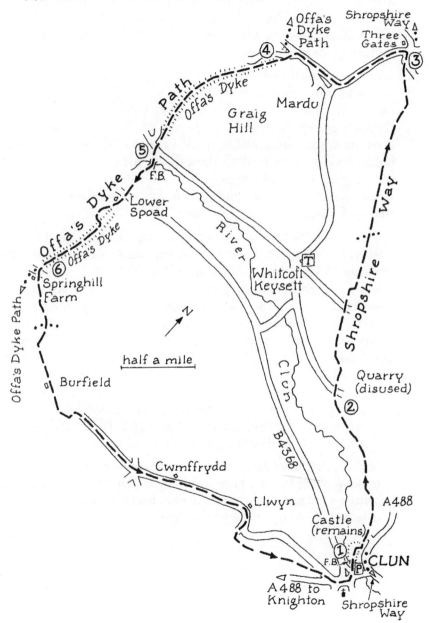

Hill (not descending towards the lane), noting in particular the lovely view up the valley towards Newcastle with a church in the foreground. The path then descends steeply towards the River Clun, crossing a lane, to reach and cross the substantial footbridge over the river.

5. Walk upstream and then alongside the fence to the right, to cross a stile in the corner of the field and pass to the left of the dyke (which was not in evidence by the river). Bear left across a lane, through a farmyard and climb out of the valley along the obvious track. Follow this track bending left over a stream before forking right to climb alongside a particularly fine section of the dyke. Continue climbing on one side or the other of the dyke to pass through a handgate on the crest of the hill, emerging onto a lane by Springhill Farm.

6. Go through the left-hand gate opposite, leaving the trail, to descend diagonally. Continue in the same direction in the ensuing fields to pass through a handgate at a junction of bridleways. Bear right diagonally across the next field to pass through the gate in the corner and join a track in an enchanting little valley. Follow this track for a mile through a farm to cross-roads. Turn left along a quiet lane, signposted to Clun, to continue the very gradual descent. Turn right up a track by Peartree Cottage, go on through a handgate and turn left along the side of an old stone cottage. Continue the descent along an enclosed green lane. Cross a metal stile and go straight on down a stony track, at the end of which, bear right. Turn left down the main road, unless deviating to view the church.

St George's Church has suffered extensive Victorian restoration but some Norman features have survived, most notably the tower and columns in the nave. Indeed the massive tower may have been a defensive feature pre-dating the castle.

Walk 24: Cwm-sanaham Hill an Knucklas from Lloyney

Starting point: Grid reference 244759, lay-by adjacent to the Lloyney I... on the B4355 about 3.5 miles north-west of Knighton

Distance: 8 miles (12.9 kilometres)

Height gain: 1700 feet (520 metres)

Relevant maps: Explorer 201 (Knighton and Presteigne), Landranger 137 (Ludlow, Wenlock Edge)

Facilities: Full facilities in Knighton, inns in Lloyney and Knucklas

Terrain: Field paths, tracks and quiet country lanes. There are some very soft stretches. The walk includes a steeply undulating length of the Offa's Dyke Trail after a long but gradual climb up to the trail. There is another climb up between Knucklas Castle and the railway viaduct nearing the end of the walk, which is therefore one of the most strenuous described in this book. This last climb can be avoided by continuing along the lane, signposted to Lloyney, mentioned in paragraph 4.

The Jack Mytton Way, utilised in part on this walk, is a bridleway extending some 70 miles over the Shropshire Hills between Llanfair Waterdine and Highley. It includes the particularly attractive Long Mynd and Wenlock Edge. "Mad Jack" Mytton was a gentleman of the county and enthusiastic horseman whose exploits made him a legend in his lifetime.

1. Cross the road and walk up the lane opposite, signposted to Llanfair Waterdine, to a T-junction and turn right. Turn left up a waymarked track by the side of "Nantiago", crossing the stile at the top of the track and go forward up the side of a field. As the field levels out turn right over a stile and turn right along a bridleway between hedges. Ignore the gully to the left and continue, between the sparsely populated hedges, to pass a marker post at the top edge of woodland. Bear left through two handgates to join another bridleway, initially enclosed, and then between stunted trees to a junction of tracks.

2. Turn left up an enclosed stony track for over half a mile , bearing

The fortified railway viaduct straddling the village of Knucklas

right past a large farm, to a junction of bridleways. Carry straight on, over a cattle grid, up the major track to a T-junction at the top of the hill, having breached Offa's Dyke. Turn right down a track, joining the trail for about two miles. This track continues alongside the dyke, having breached it yet again. Bear left through the farm in the valley, cross a lane and footbridge over a stream. Continue along the dyke over another footbridge to cross the shoulder of a hill, where the path is punctuated by marker posts. Descend steeply to cross a lane and follow the clear track ahead past "Brynorgan".

3. Climb steeply up to and alongside a wire fence, cross a stile to bear left past a marker post and follow another fence to a trig point.

> *This is the top of Cwm-sanaham Hill, a superb viewpoint which seems far higher than a mere 406 metres – the switchback route of the Offa's Dyke Trail has certainly required a disproportionate effort to reach this height!*

4. Turn left to start the initially steep descent past isolated conifers. Cross a stony track and contour along the side of the hill

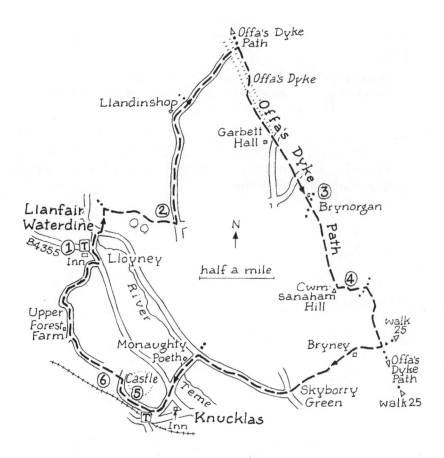

below forestry. Carry on along the top edge of a field and turn right down the next cross-track, leaving the trail. At a junction of tracks by "The Brynny", go straight on through a gate beside the cottage and rejoin the track which descends to a junction of lanes. Turn right along the lane, signposted to Lloyney, and turn left at the next junction to the main road. Cross this road and bear left along a lane towards Knucklas Village Centre. Turn right, by the telephone box, up a narrow lane converging with the viaduct.

The massive railway viaduct with 13 stone arches and turrets at both ends was constructed late in the 19th century.

5. Carry on briefly where the lane degenerates to a track and on the next bend turn left through a gate to proceed up the left side of a field.

Knucklas Castle, superbly sited in the early 13ᵗʰ century, was destroyed by the Welsh later in the same century and nothing remains today other than the earthworks.

6. Walk straight on up an enclosed green lane at the end of which turn right down a track which winds downhill, developing into a lane, to the main road. Turn left to return to the lay-by which is just around the bend in the road.

Walk 25: Five Turnings and Holloway Rocks from Knighton

Starting point: Grid reference 288722, car park by the bus station on the north side of Bridge Street in Knighton

Distance: 8 miles (12.9 kilometres)

Height gain: 1100 feet (330 metres)

Relevant maps: Explorer 201 (Knighton and Presteigne), Landranger 137 (Ludlow, Wenlock Edge)

Facilities: Full facilities in Knighton

Terrain: Principally good, clear, firm tracks and consequently easy route finding. After a short steep climb out of Knighton the walk continues gently uphill to Holloway Rocks before the progressive descent into Knighton. It is essential to find the broad, safe track winding down the face of Holloway Rocks.

Knighton is the administrative centre of the Offa's Dyke Trail, which many consider synonymous with the mid-point of the trail. Those walking the linear trail from south to north may therefore be surprised to find they still have 97 miles to walk to Prestatyn – distinctly further than the distance previously covered. The less than gentle undulations of the path north of Knighton also generates the most testing walking of the whole trail. The town has a clock tower reminiscent of Hay-on-Wye, and the mounds of two old castles. St. Edward's Church has been greatly restored but the 14th century west tower remains, and there is a medieval cruck-built house at the top of Broad Street (behind the more modern façade). Most buildings are Victorian and many are care-worn for lack of maintenance.

1. Walk along the main street towards the Offa's Dyke Centre, passing the clocktower. Turn right through the grounds of the centre, following the Offa's Dyke Trail down to the bank of the River Teme. Turn left upstream to cross the river, by way of the footbridge by the railway, and turn left over the line to continue walking upstream. Turn right at the next finger post, to cross a stile by a gate and bear left across a lane.

The Offa's Dyke Centre, passed at the start of the walk

2. Climb steeply up the track opposite, which soon degenerates to a path climbing alongside woodland. Nearing the top of the hill turn left, as indicated by a finger post, and just before reaching a stile. Cross a track to continue uphill, alongside conifers and the dyke, then carry on along the clearer path joined by a wire fence on the right. Climb the first of a series of stiles, where there are glorious views up the valley dominated by the massive railway viaduct at Knucklas and an aerial view of Knighton. Continue over stiles and pass above two barns. 200 metres further on turn right along a track, which is a waymarked bridleway, leaving the Offa's Dyke Trail. Go forward between hedges and then alongside a fence to the right, through trees. Leaving the fence, descend diagonally across a huge field towards a farm. Pass through the gate in the bottom corner to proceed, between hedges, and cross the Clun - Knighton road.

3. Walk on along a very straight track, to the right of Five Turnings Farm, for about one and a half miles – the first half of which is enclosed, then along the edge of fields and between conifer

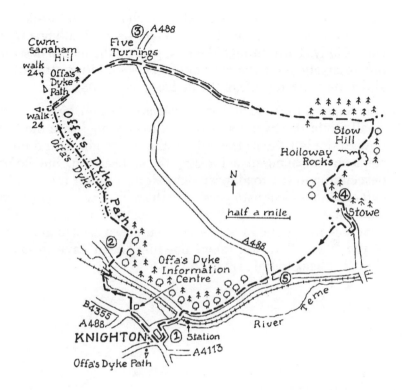

plantations. Approaching a pond turn right to cross a large field, as indicated by a finger post adjacent to a stile in the fence on the left. Cresting the rise, where there is a glorious panoramic view of the Teme Valley and Knighton, bear right. Find the broad stony track and follow it winding down a cleft in Holloway Rocks. Continue along the principal track bending right past a pond before descending again to, and through, forestry to Stowe Church.

> *St. Michael and All Angels is a medieval church, with impressive exposed roof timbers, which has not been spoilt by Victorian restorers. The now sleepy hamlet of Stowe was historically of some significance having been at a junction of drovers' roads.*

4. Turn right down a lane past the church and, immediately after passing a farm, turn right opposite a letterbox, along an enclosed track. After 70 metres turn right through a gate and walk up a field, to pass through another gate and bear left along a track very briefly. Turn through the next gate on the left, to descend progressively along the bottom of fields, and then straight on along the opposite side of the hedge to the A488.

5. Bear left over the road to cross a field as indicated, by way of the small footbridge over a stream, and to converge with the road now to the left. Cross the stile in the hedge ahead and climb steps to the bend in a forestry track. Bear left, but before descending to the road, bear right along a minor track which extends into a clear path parallel to the road. Emerging from the woodland onto the road by Knighton Station, cross the bridge over the railway and River Teme and proceed back to the centre of the town. Turn left down Bowling Green Lane to take a short-cut back to the car park.

Also of interest:

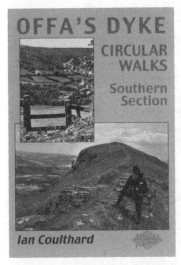

OFFA'S DYKE CIRCULAR WALKS: SOUTHERN SECTION
Ian Coulthard
The companion to *Offa's Dyke Circular Walks: Northern Section*, and details another 25 energetic circular day-walks based on the Offa's Dyke long-distance trail between Knighton and Chepstow. The walks average 9 miles in length and involve a height gain of up to 2000 ft. The routes incorporate many historic sites such as Tintern Abbey, Llanthony Priory, White Castle and the border towns. £7.95

SNOWDONIA ROCKY RAMBLES
Bryan Lynas
This sequel to *Lakeland Rocky Rambles*, with a Foreword by James Lovelock FRS, is much more than a book of mountain walks. Each of the ten is a voyage of discovery and a journey through time, with insights into the geology, wildlife and history of these splendid peaks. £9.95

NORTH WALES WALKING ON THE LEVEL
Norman Buckley
25 circular walks in the hills and mountains of North Wales, for those who enjoy gentle walking in fine surroundings but do not wish to make significant ascents. Route maps, descriptions of towns and villages, landscape and interesting features are all included. There is a summary of each walk, including length and total ascent. £6.95

BEST TEA SHOP WALKS IN SNOWDONIA
Dorothy Hamilton
Enjoy a leisurely ramble in beautiful Snowdonia and complete the experience with Welsh afternoon tea at a recommended tea room! Walk Conwy mountain, explore Gwydr Forest and its lakes, or stroll in the Lledr and Ffestiniog valleys. £6.95
NOTE: "Best Tea Shop Walks" by Dorothy Hamilton are available for Lleyn & Anglesey, The Clwydian Hills & Welsh Borderlands, and South & West Wales – all £6.95 each

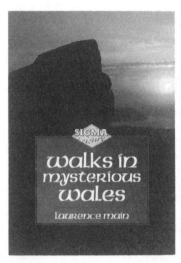

WALKING THE BRECON BEACONS AND THE BLACK MOUNTAINS
David Hunter
This is a collection of circular walks in the Brecon Beacons National Park "...the most comprehensive collection of walks produced for the locality" POWYS COUNTY TIMES £7.95

WALKS IN MYSTERIOUS WALES
Laurence Main
Ley hunter and researcher Laurence Main has compiled a vast collection of folklore and walks for his readers. "An excellent book" GLAMORGAN GAZETTE. "Most informative" CAMBRIAN NEWS. £6.95

BEST PUB WALKS IN SNOWDONIA
Laurence Main
A strenuous hike up Snowdon, or a leisurely amble in the foothills. There's a huge variety here, with the assurance of a welcome from the hillsides for weary walkers. £6.95

SNOWDONIA WALKS WITH CHILDREN
Nick Lambert
20, circular walks designed with children in mind, and covering the whole of Snowdonia. Some routes feature well-known beauty spots, others quieter, lesser-frequented areas where it is possible to 'get away from it all' and enjoy the peace of the countryside. Includes questions (with answers) and features to spot along the way. £6.95

HILL WALKS IN MID WALES: The Cambrian Mountains
Dave Ing
There's more to Wales than Snowdonia. Discover the true heart of Wales - "David's book will not have a successor" WESTERN MAIL. £8.95

All of our books are available through booksellers. In case of difficulty, or for a free catalogue, contact:
SIGMA LEISURE, 1 SOUTH OAK LANE, WILMSLOW, CHESHIRE SK9 6AR.
Phone: 01625-531035 Fax: 01625-536800. E-mail: info@sigmapress.co.uk
Web site: http//www.sigmapress.co.uk MASTERCARD and VISA orders welcome.